EXAM Revision NOTES

A2 GOVERNMENT & POLITICS
Political Ideologies

Daniel Woodley

Series Editor: Eric Magee

2nd Edition

Philip Allan Updates, an imprint of Hodder Education, an Hachette UK company, Market Place, Deddington, Oxfordshire OX15 0SE

Orders

Bookpoint Ltd, 130 Milton Park, Abingdon, Oxfordshire OX14 4SB
tel: 01235 827720
fax: 01235 400454
e-mail: uk.orders@bookpoint.co.uk

Lines are open 9 a.m.–5 p.m., Monday to Saturday, with a 24-hour message answering service. You can also order through the Philip Allan Updates website: www.philipallan.co.uk

© Philip Allan Updates 2009

ISBN 978-0-340-99080-3

First printed 2009
Impression number   5   4   3   2   1
Year   2014   2013   2012   2011   2010   2009

Printed in Spain

Environmental information
Hachette UK's policy is to use papers that are natural, renewable and recyclable products and made from wood grown in sustainable forests. The logging and manufacturing processes are expected to conform to the environmental regulations of the country of origin.

Contents

Introduction

Using this textbook

This revision guide is intended for students sitting A2 Government and Politics (Edexcel Topic B/AQA route B). Each chapter is devoted to a specific ideology, based on an analysis of key concepts in that tradition and contains a summary of the principal arguments and debates in political theory relevant to the study of ideologies. Key terms and concepts appear in bold in the text and are defined at the end of each chapter. This book is not intended to serve as a substitute for independent study. You will need to have completed the A2 course in an appropriate educational setting with instruction from a qualified teacher. While every attempt has been made to present the material in a systematic, logical format, this guide is not intended to be an exhaustive text.

What is ideology?

The term 'ideology' is one of the more slippery concepts in the social sciences. We have all heard the term, and we all use it from time to time, yet few people understand what it means, perhaps because it has so many possible meanings. The cultural theorist Professor Terry Eagleton lists some of these possible meanings, including:

- action-oriented sets of beliefs (political mobilisation);
- a body of ideas characteristic of a particular social group or class;
- ideas which help to legitimate a dominant social power;
- false ideas which help to legitimate a dominant social power (false consciousness);
- distorted communication;
- forms of thought motivated by social interests;
- utopian thought; and
- the medium through which individuals make sense of their world.

Which definition is correct? The best way to differentiate between possible meanings of the term is to classify them into two broad categories: social-scientific approaches, and critical Marxist approaches.

Social-scientific approaches

It was the French philosopher Antoine Destutt de Tracy (1754–1836) who coined the term 'ideology'. De Tracy envisaged the study of ideology as a positive science, i.e. as an empirical study of the determinants of ideas. He believed, like many eighteenth-century rationalists, that if philosophers could discover how and why people arrive at their ideas and beliefs, then they could develop techniques for promoting a 'correct' form of consciousness. This view is based on the assumption that ideologies are like any other social phenomenon that can be studied in an objective and scientific way. For this reason, de Tracy is seen as the first 'scientist of ideas'. One thinker who adapted this approach was Karl Mannheim (1893–1947). He differentiated between:

- ideologies as 'system ideas' (which contribute to social integration and the stabilisation of political systems); and
- 'utopias' (which are adopted by opposition groups in their struggle against the existing social order).

Mannheim concluded that it is intellectuals who act as the 'carriers' or 'disseminators' of ideologies because only educated or cosmopolitan individuals are able to break free of the dominant values of their own social environment. As an idealist, he believed it would ultimately be possible to develop an appropriate ideological worldview to promote social integration and value-consensus. This rationalistic perspective reflects an enduring belief, within Western social science, in the possibility of social engineering.

Critical Marxist approaches

The philosopher Karl Marx (1818–83) rejected the prevailing view that ideas are the driving force of history. He argued that it is not consciousness that determines human social life but social life that determines consciousness. In his view, ideas do not exist independently of man's existence; they do not simply come into being in a random or arbitrary way. Rather, the nature of human thought is determined by the social and historical context in which it originated.

For this reason, Marx is known as a historical materialist, and the basic principle underlying his conception of ideology is that all ideas — and therefore all forms of ideology — are expressions of a particular historical time. Individuals and groups produce ideas in accordance with their interests, and dominant ideologies tend to reflect the values of the dominant social class.

However, Marx was also concerned with the way ideology distorts reality, thereby helping to conceal the social contradictions in society. What this means is that political ideas that appear to have a timeless, natural quality (as 'given for all time') are more often than not a version of reality that suits the interests of the ruling class. Dominant ideologies may appeal to universal 'truths', e.g. that formal equality is a necessary and sufficient guarantee of political freedom, but this also reflects the 'truth' as it is defined by those who benefit from a particular set of social arrangements. For some disadvantaged groups, this leads to 'false consciousness', i.e. to a mistaken identification with the values of the ruling class.

For Marxists, therefore, ideology is used to conceal the contradictions in class society by promoting 'false consciousness' among the masses in the interests of political stability and social integration. Later Marxists such as Lenin developed this critical perspective by defining ideologies as forms of political consciousness linked to different social classes. Lenin's view of ideology is important because it provided the basis for a redefinition of ideology among the Communist movement during the twentieth century. Whereas Marx viewed ideology critically, Lenin differentiated between 'negative' bourgeois and 'positive' socialist ideology. This helped pave the way for a degeneration of ideology in the Soviet Union into little more than propaganda.

Criticisms of Marx's theory of ideology

There are three major problems with Marx's theory of false consciousness, which tends to underestimate the positive function of ideologies:

- Marx failed to see that some workers identify with the ideas of the ruling class for conscious, self-interested motives rather than because they are victims of necessary 'false consciousness'; at the very least people are fatalistic rather than completely stupid, and if they cannot change the world they have little choice but to cooperate with the system.

- All ideologies say something positive about how we view the world. For this reason, ideologies specify a particular view of human nature, of what human beings are capable of achieving. Some political ideologies, e.g. liberalism, are more optimistic and some, e.g. conservatism, are more pessimistic. Either way, all ideologies embody a world-view that helps to define the direction of social and political action.

- All social groups produce ideologies to help identify their needs and legitimise their interests. Although the mainstream values and beliefs in society reflect the interests of the economically dominant social class, there are also competing ideologies, e.g. feminism and ecologism, that challenge the mainstream. If one single set of ideas were so all-powerful, then politics would never progress.

Gramsci's concept of 'hegemony'

In contrast to Marx and Lenin, Antonio Gramsci (1891–1937) developed a theory of ideology that avoids the problem of false consciousness by focusing on the link between ideology and class domination. Unlike Lenin, who understood ideology as a means for deceiving the masses (under capitalism) or mobilising the masses (under socialism), Gramsci sought to explain how ideology sustains the ascendancy of one particular type of class society by projecting its specific values as timeless and universal.

He explained this in terms of the concept 'hegemony', which can be defined broadly as:

> The ways in which social, political, religious and legal institutions reproduce the power of the ruling class through the promotion of ideological consensus. Hegemony cannot be understood simply as a function of coercion, for all stable political systems require consent. It is through the manufacture of consent over time that dominant groups are able to legitimate their rule, such that the political order assumes a kind of 'taken for granted' status.

While Gramsci's theory of hegemony is an improvement on earlier conceptions of ideology, it has been surpassed by more recent approaches, which stress the different meanings ideologies hold for individuals and social groups in their daily lives. A more sophisticated way to view ideology is to see it in terms of discourse. Gramsci concentrates on the dominant ideology in society as a hegemonic system of values and beliefs. But in any society there are likely to be competing forms of discourse that produce specific 'social effects' or ways of being.

According to Pierre Bourdieu (1930–2002), individuals internalise ideological ways of being and thinking, which become like 'second nature' and which have a determining effect on social action. What this means in practice is that ideology cannot simply

be reduced in the Marxist sense to an expression of economic interests, nor can it be seen in a purely rationalist sense as a conscious, well-organised system of beliefs. Both concepts ignore the affective and symbolic dimensions of ideologies — the way ideologies help to shape people's experience and their relationship to structures of power in society.

Summary

Ideologies influence how subjects think and act, but also allow individuals to express their needs and interests in a political context. The main functions of ideology are mobilisation, legitimation and representation.

Mobilisation

Ideologies mobilise groups behind political goals. Mobilisation is a positive function of ideology because political action requires commitment and participation. Without ideology, groups lack a clear political profile. Social organisation is a complex and variable phenomenon, and one of the basic functions of ideology is to codify and express the shared concepts and values of social groups while excluding alternative concepts and values as inappropriate and/or deviant.

Legitimation

As Marxists argue, ideologies also serve to legitimise the economic and social interests of powerful groups. Ruling-class ideologies favour those interests that are supportive of the system, while marginalising those interests that seek to change the status quo.

Representation

Ideologies specify a particular way of looking at the world, and help to translate vague ideas and beliefs into political goals. Ideologies give shape to everyday experience and reinforce identities. It is essential to bear in mind that ideologies are representations of social reality that are adopted by social groups in pursuit of specific goals, whether in defence of existing interests, e.g. conservatism, or as an instrument to transform social reality, e.g. socialism or feminism.

1 Liberalism

1 Introduction

Liberalism is a core topic in the A2 specification (Edexcel Unit 3B; AQA Unit 3B; OCR Unit F854). To succeed at A2, you must be able to differentiate clearly between classical and modern liberalism, between negative freedom and positive freedom, and between mainstream liberalism and libertarianism. You must also be familiar with the principal thinkers in the liberal tradition, and current debates over the future of neoliberalism.

Liberalism is based on a set of **normative** and descriptive theories concerning the proper relationship between the state, the individual and society.

- On the one hand, liberals advocate individualism, freedom, toleration and constitutionalism; they believe that the scope of government should be limited, and should not undermine the autonomy, privacy and choice of individuals who are bound to one another through voluntary or contractual ties rather than through culture or tradition.
- On the other hand, liberals oppose ideas, beliefs and institutions not founded on **rational** principles: progress is linked to enlightened reform, and to the free development of education and science.

There is also a close link between liberalism and capitalism. Part of the appeal of liberalism is that it is compatible with both economic freedom and **democracy**. Although liberalism is often described as the 'dominant ideology of the West', liberal ideas have exercised a major impact on the development of political systems throughout the modern world.

However, as Professor John Gray argues, there is a tension running through liberalism between its two rival traditions. On the one hand, classical liberals advocate a genuinely pluralist model of social and political organisation based on peaceful coexistence between different regimes and ways of life, where the state assumes a morally neutral stance between competing values and beliefs. On the other hand, modern liberals believe in the possibility of a universal rational consensus, where the state actively promotes specific ways of life considered to be valuable and worthwhile.

Key issues and debates
- **the normative grounds of individualism;**
- **the distinction between negative and positive freedom;**
- **economic liberalism;**
- **the implications of individualism for the state;**
- **the nature and limits of liberal toleration;**
- **the tensions between liberalism and democracy;**
- **modern liberalism and social reform;**
- **the continuity between classical liberalism and neoliberalism; and**
- **liberalism and civil liberties.**

2 Core ideas of liberalism

2.1 Rationalism

All ideologies specify a particular view of human nature. When we consider the influence of human nature, we are concerned primarily with the essential character of mankind — what human beings are capable of achieving, and which forms of political organisation are most conducive to the formation of stable and prosperous human communities.

Liberalism is based on an optimistic faith in human nature and the capacity of mankind to behave rationally. Unlike conservatives, liberals believe that all knowledge and beliefs can be explained by the exercise of reason alone. This reflects their faith in **Enlightenment** reason: humans possess the capacity to shape their world by acting in accordance with agreed rules and procedures. Social and political problems can be resolved in the same way as scientific questions, by employing rational methods and techniques.

Note Liberalism is defined by a belief in and commitment to rationality. This assumption is central to classical political economy and modern neoliberalism.

2.2 Individualism

Whereas socialists focus on the community or the group, liberals hold an 'atomistic' view of society as an aggregation of individuals. Individuals are understood to possess rights to life, liberty and property, and liberal thinkers argue that society should be organised so as to promote diversity and the free development of individuality. This perspective is an expression of the increasing economic and social freedom of members of the educated class in the eighteenth and nineteenth centuries, as writers, artists and philosophers questioned the social constraints on individual liberty and freedom of expression.

However, liberals advocate individuality not just for its own sake, but because individuality and diversity are preconditions of progress. As the utilitarian philosopher John Stuart Mill (1806–73) wrote in *On Liberty*:

'Where, not the person's own character, but the traditions or customs of other people are the rule of conduct, there is wanting one of the principal ingredients of human happiness, and quite the chief ingredient of individuals and social progress.'

Individualism is also viewed as a central feature of **liberal democracy**, which is concerned above all with reconciling the rights of individuals with the will of the majority. This finds expression in the liberal emphasis on **constitutionalism** as a means for reducing concentrations of power, protecting minorities, and lessening political interference in the private affairs of **civil society**.

2.3 Freedom

Belief in freedom is a cardinal principle of all liberal ideologies, stemming back to the late seventeenth century. John Locke (1632–1704) believed that personal liberty and freedom to own property are essential features of civilised societies, and that all individuals should voluntarily give their **consent** to be governed (if only tacitly). This outlook is also reflected in the work of Mill, who insisted that 'the only purpose for which power can be rightly exercised over any member of a civilised community, against his will, is to prevent harm to others'.

All liberals value freedom as a condition for the free development of individuals. However, there is an important distinction between 'negative freedom' and 'positive freedom':

- In classical liberalism, freedom is understood in a 'negative sense' as freedom from coercion. Classical liberals do not define freedom in a substantive way (as the freedom to do one thing rather than another), but maintain that people are free if and only if they possess a 'sphere of non-interference' that cannot be violated by external powers such as the state. For classical liberals, the only freedom that is seen as worthy of the name is the freedom of each individual to pursue his or her own conception of 'good' in his or her own way, unhindered by others.
- In modern liberalism, on the other hand, freedom is understood in a 'positive' sense as empowerment. 'New liberals' such as T. H. Green (1836–82) argued that freedom from coercion is inadequate unless all individuals are free to develop their talents and energies unhindered by poverty, illiteracy, disease or injustice. However, this emphasis on empowerment as a condition for true freedom implies a greater role for the state in determining which of the many competing goals in society should be pursued to promote the welfare of the majority of citizens.

2.4 Rights and justice

Justice refers to the fair treatment of people. Liberals believe in the equal worth of all individuals ('foundational **equality**'), and that all individuals are equal before the law ('formal equality'). They understand justice in a procedural sense, i.e. as a rules-based system for adjudicating between rival claims rather than for privileging a specific definition of the 'good'. From this perspective, legal and political institutions should adopt a *neutral* rather than an *activist* position when making judgements or framing legislation, allowing the law and the state to act as neutral arbiters.

However, this view has been criticised by those who believe that rules *themselves* are inseparable from specific ways of life. Critics of liberalism stress that rules and procedures always involve prior acceptance of certain substantive ethical commitments. In this way, the content of social practices impacts on the nature of rules — rules that may be presented as value-free, but that are in fact the product of specific cultures.

The liberal conception of justice is also exemplified by the idea of equal rights. People should have an equal opportunity to demonstrate their worth. This leads to the idea of 'meritocracy', where the most talented rise to the top by virtue of superior talents. As Professor Joseph Raz argues, rights are effectively the basis of duties in others, and respecting people's rights means giving appropriate weight to their interests.

However, there is some debate about whether rights occur 'naturally' or flow from membership of a specific polity:
- *Natural rights theorists* such as Professor Ronald Dworkin argue that respect for individuals' rights is the foundation of political morality. He treats rights as 'trumps', which override competing considerations. Collective goals cannot be used to justify denying individuals the right to do what they wish or for imposing some loss or injury on them.
- *Legal positivists*, on the other hand, maintain that individuals have rights only insofar as these are recognised and codified within legal systems. This view is closer to the reality of modern societies in which the structure and content of law undergo a process of 'systemisation'.

Despite the increasing systemisation of law, the natural rights tradition remains an important feature of Western political theory, because it assumes that humans are by nature rational and good, and that they carry into political society those rights that they enjoyed in earlier stages of history. This view is held particularly strongly by libertarians and philosophical anarchists.

2.5 Toleration

Liberals favour toleration and respect for the opinions of others, and reject prejudice and intolerance. Toleration implies *forbearance*, the quality of being patient and sympathetic towards others' views or conduct, even if these views or conduct are unappealing. Voltaire (1694–1778) famously championed the rights of religious and political dissenters, even those whose views horrify us. Toleration is, he suggested, 'the consequence of humanity. We are all formed of frailty and error; let us pardon reciprocally each other's folly, that is the first law of nature'.

The concept of toleration was developed most fully by Mill, who advocated freedom of thought and discussion, stressing the utility of contradictory opinions even where they are manifestly erroneous: 'If all mankind minus one were of one opinion,' he argued, 'mankind would be no more justified in silencing that one person than he, if he had the power, would be justified in silencing mankind.' In other words, mankind benefits from **pluralism** rather than conformism because social progress is undermined wherever dissenting opinions are repressed.

What is destroyed in the suppression of alternative views is not just the distinctiveness or diversity of those views, but the possibility of new ways of thinking and seeing, so that we are robbed of the opportunity either to falsify our existing beliefs or to verify what we hold to be true. As long as we can agree on basic principles of justice, alternative beliefs and ways of life should be respected precisely because they challenge received prejudices and force us to rethink our cherished ideas.

Mill concedes that new or radical ideas may be rejected because society fears change or may be insecure about its beliefs; but even if new ideas disturb us, we must give them a fair hearing because the assumption of moral certainty or infallibility is usually based on arrogance, self-interest or self-delusion.

3 *Classical liberalism*

Classical liberalism is a term used to refer to a political school of thought in which primary emphasis is placed on securing the freedom of the individual by limiting the power of social groups to manipulate social outcomes through the state. In its economic form, it advocates a respect for private property and free markets. In its political form, it advocates pluralism and toleration, although early classical liberals such as Locke retained a specific vision of the type of rational community they wished to promote, which excluded forms of association considered inappropriate to the maintenance of limited government.

Classical liberals remain sceptical of democracy as a value in itself, believing that too much democracy can undermine property freedom or lead to political instability. In this sense, one can be a liberal without being in favour of egalitarian democracy.

3.1 Possessive individualism

Locke's political philosophy is informed by his understanding of the institution of private property, which lies at the heart of classical liberal ideology. Locke argued that individuals' right to property should be based on the labour that each person invests to create that property from the state of nature. He insisted that 'God gave the world to the use of the industrious and rational', and this view has been crucial to the development of liberal ideology since the eighteenth century. However, in liberal

Classical liberalism

ideology, property is not only the right of all those who labour to create it. It also provides individuals with a resource to defend themselves against the encroaching power of the state because despotic power can only be exercised over those who are without property.

C. B. Macpherson (1911–87) defined liberalism as an ideology based on 'possessive individualism', a political school of thought he traced back to the work of Thomas Hobbes (1588–1679) and Locke. In its simplest form, possessive individualism implies that all individuals possess or acquire skills and resources that are their exclusive property: they do not owe a debt to society for endowments that can be exchanged for other resources in the open market. This theory of liberty has two fundamental consequences:

- it establishes the principle of exclusive private ownership, grounding bourgeois property freedom in law; and
- it connects political rights to economic resources: legitimate ownership of property symbolises rights in a concrete form.

Supporters of possessive individualism argue that it provides a utilitarian basis for the type of commercial civilisation that emerged in Western Europe in the eighteenth century, a society founded on contractual rather than affective bonds or communal obligations. However, critics maintain that it replaces alternative justifications for social action based on non-utilitarian calculation. In either event, possessive individualism constitutes the philosophical core of classical liberalism, underpinning the ideological assumptions that society is comprised of rational individuals interacting through market relations, that individuals should take precedence over the collective, and that the proper function of the state should be restricted to providing security and guaranteeing the free operation of the market.

Following Locke, the economist and philosopher Adam Smith (1723–90) was concerned with the relative importance of social and selfish motives for human conduct. According to Smith, social order also derives from the activity of self-interested rational actors:

'It is not from the benevolence of the butcher, the brewer or the baker that we expect our dinner,' he argued, 'but from their regard for their own interest.'

Smith tried to reconcile the self-interested nature of human beings with the prevailing view of the individual as a moral agent. He concluded that, by acting according to the dictates of their moral faculties, individuals by necessity pursue the 'most effective means for promoting the happiness of mankind', and that, through the unintended consequences of their own actions, they increase the total sum of human welfare.

In other words, through the 'invisible hand' of the market, which allocates resources in accordance with the relative worth of human goals, people are led to promote useful ends that were not necessarily their original intentions. This economic–philosophical argument has been used by liberal economists to justify:

- economic self-interest;
- unrestricted free enterprise;
- limited state intervention;
- anti-welfarism; and
- low taxation.

The classical liberal view is indeed extremely important because it has major implications for the liberal conception of the state. Classical liberals believe that the purpose of government is not to organise the economic activities of citizens or to define the correct purpose of social life, but to regulate and defend the institution of property, and to create the conditions for the development of private commerce and trade.

However, once it is accepted that individuals possess an unequal endowment of resources, it is clear that property rights become an important determinant of social and political relations. For this reason, socialists criticise economic liberalism because it appears to do nothing to address the undeserved social and natural inequalities that determine individuals' life-chances.

Note Marx argued that Adam Smith sought to legitimise capitalism by distorting the true nature of accumulation: capitalism *appears* to generate surplus value through exchange, but the real source of wealth is *labour*.

3.2 Liberalism and the state

Classical liberals are strong supporters of constitutional government, placing legal restrictions on the exercise of sovereign power. Constitutionalism may be defined as respect for principles and established legal precedents in the organisation of political systems. In Europe and North America, this has been characterised by the development of representative democracy and universal suffrage, which enable citizens to elect legislators and to remove incompetent or corrupt rulers. The purpose of constitutional government is to provide political authority with a normative framework, which in turn provides a basis for **political obligation**.

The consent theory of obligation

Constitutional government is based first and foremost on the principle of consent. To demonstrate the need for a contract (or 'covenant') between the individual and the state, Hobbes pointed to the asocial and anarchic nature of human society as it exists in a 'state of nature'. He defined a 'state of nature' as the pre-political condition of mankind before the creation of stable institutions of government. Under such conditions, he argued, human social life is reduced to a 'war of all against all', in which existence becomes 'solitary, poor, nasty, brutish and short'. The only remedy for this situation is for citizens to submit to the power of an absolute sovereign.

However, Locke argues that Hobbes' absolutism fails because by giving up their rights to an all-powerful sovereign, individuals are no more secure than they would have been in a state of nature. In order to protect citizens from an authoritarian sovereign, civil society must be defended. For Locke, a civil society can only come into being where:

- citizens voluntarily hand over their individual power to take the law into their own hands, and government is based on the *consent of the governed*;
- the state represents the rule of the majority; and
- rulers divorce their own private interests from their official powers and duties.

Locke argued that every effort should be made to ensure that those who wield power do not develop interests separate from the interests of the community. Should this occur, he argued, then citizens have a right to withdraw their consent because it is up to the people to judge whether their rulers have acted contrary to the trust invested in them.

Although the idea of consent has been challenged by critics of liberalism and individuals are rarely, if ever, asked if they consider a system of government to be just or

unjust, the assumption of consent between rulers and ruled provides the basis of political legitimacy in liberal–democratic systems.

Note Consent and obligation are two sides of the same coin. Once consent is given, citizens in democratic states are assumed to have an unconditional obligation to obey the law.

3.3 Constitutional mechanisms

The principles of consent and obligation are only one aspect of constitutional government. In liberal ideology, no democracy can be considered safe if the activities of government are not subject to a system of checks and balances designed to prevent abuses of power. Although liberals stress the capacity of humans to act in accordance with reason, there is a strong current of realism in liberal ideology, as expressed in the historian Lord Acton's dictum, 'Power tends to corrupt, and absolute power corrupts absolutely'. The American president and thinker Thomas Jefferson (1743–1826) argued that democracy must also be based on a system of constitutional mechanisms. These include:

- the **rule of law**, to ensure that governments do not abuse the powers of office;
- free and fair elections, to allow the electorate to choose their rulers;
- a codified constitution incorporating a bill of rights;
- **separation of powers**, to ensure that the executive branch of government is subject to a formal system of checks and balances;
- a bicameral legislature, with one chamber to represent the electorate and a second chamber to represent regional interests; and
- federalism, where regional authorities 'pool' their sovereignty to create a higher level of government with executive **authority** to act in the interests of the member states.

The ultimate purpose of constitutional government is, therefore, to prevent concentrations of power. In liberal–democratic states, constitutional mechanisms function as safeguards to prevent rulers from abusing their power, and to protect the legal rights and freedoms of citizens. Although rulers can pass enabling legislation to override constitutional safeguards, such forms of intervention are normally used only in times of national emergency.

3.4 Liberalism and democracy

Liberalism is based on a *procedural* rather than *substantive* concept of democracy, in which restrictions are placed on the scope of government. Early liberals such as Mill and Alexis de Tocqueville (1805–59) were sceptical of majoritarian democracy because this meant potentially placing power in the hands of the uneducated classes, who could use their numerical strength to override the interests of elites. For this reason, liberals oppose radical forms of democracy based on the 'general will', which, they argue, provide inadequate safeguards against tyranny.

For liberals, democracy should be 'limited' and the will of the people 'mediated' through the people's representatives. Unlike socialists, who believe in **popular sovereignty**, liberals separate the formal institutions of democratic government from their content by reducing democratic government to its decision-making procedures and forms of organisation. In liberal societies, rules apply concerning the range and extent of legislation, and many areas of social and economic life lie outside the scope of politics. However, the intuitive assumption that liberalism and democracy are compatible is not as obvious as it seems, and some critics suggest that liberal democracy is a contradiction in terms, for the following reasons:

Liberal democracy is too restrictive

Liberal–democratic theory rests on the principle of formal equality, which states that all citizens have an equal right to vote and an equal right to influence political outcomes. However, critics argue that there is a contradiction in liberal democracy because, although voters have an equal opportunity to influence the choice of government, they have neither an equal understanding of the issues nor an equal opportunity to influence the outcome of elections.

The principle of democratic equality embodied in the slogan 'one person, one vote' conceals the very unequal power of resource-rich actors such as banks and corporations, which are not addressed by giving citizens equal voting rights. If democracy is to be viable, then it must compensate for the political consequences of social inequality in capitalist society, and address a wider range of economic issues, which are at present excluded from political debate.

Against this attack, liberals reply that liberal democracy is still an efficient means for reconciling individual freedom and democratic accountability. Liberal democracy implies that responsibility for *economic* decision-making belongs to the individual rather than the state: resources are allocated through competitive exchange, which does not require the same level of democratic scrutiny as *political* decision-making. Hence the definition of what counts as 'political' is reduced to those issues that cannot be resolved at the level of civil society.

There is a tension between elite rule and popular sovereignty

Critics argue that liberal democracy allows the political class to govern without meaningful participation, and to pass legislation without seeking the consent of the electorate.

Although no government can afford to ignore popular opinion for long, parliamentary sovereignty places power in the hands of a political elite rather than the people.

Yet defenders of liberalism reply that liberal democracy is the best available system for reconciling elite rule with limited popular sovereignty. The political class rules on behalf of the people who possess neither the interest nor the ability to make complex political decisions. More importantly, as de Tocqueville argued, unmediated democracy carries with it a risk that individuals and minorities may be subject to the 'tyranny of the majority'. The existence of a political class prevents continual radicalisation by allowing political leaders to channel social and economic interests into practical policy decisions.

Liberal democracy creates apathy

It is traditionally argued that, by promoting participation, liberal democracy encourages civic responsibility and political education. By allowing a free press and by not silencing dissent, liberal democracy facilitates political discussion in a way that is impossible in authoritarian or totalitarian states. Compared with their counterparts today, nineteenth-century American voters were well informed and followed the development of national and state politics closely. In comparison with the present day, this ensured higher levels of accountability and greater popular awareness and understanding of issues. Critics such as Noam Chomsky suggest that in the absence of serious media coverage of politics, voters in the United States no longer have the capacity to make informed or critical choices.

But does liberal democracy actually promote responsibility and political education? Critics point to low voter turnout and low levels of political understanding as evidence of the increasing apathy felt by many people towards politics. They suggest two reasons for this:

- Given the limited nature of politics in liberal–democratic systems, opportunities for real change are marginal, with the result that voters lose interest and leave decision-making to elites. Representative democracy has, to a greater or lesser extent, been corrupted by the power of special interests that exert disproportionate influence over the policy agenda.
- With the creation of huge media monopolies, television has 'dumbed down' coverage of political issues. As a result, serious debate has been replaced by 'infotainment', leading to the erosion of political understanding and a rapid decline in the democratic scrutiny function of the media.

It is clear that liberalism and democracy are concerned with different things. For liberals, the purpose of government is to provide a legal framework for reconciling competing interests, and the best government is that which governs least. For democrats, politics should be more than just a trade-off between interests: decisions about the determination of social goals and the allocation of resources should also be subject to democratic scrutiny.

4 *Modern liberalism*

Whereas classical liberals defend an individualist theory of social and political organisation, modern liberals argue that authentic individuality can be achieved only through community. Modern liberals insist that individuals cannot be separated from their cultural, historical and linguistic contexts, and that the real purpose of the modern state is to promote a universal rational consensus, to educate and empower citizens by promoting a specific conception of the 'public good'.

4.1 Positive freedom and the state

The philosophical origins of modern liberalism can be traced back to the German idealist tradition, principally the philosopher Hegel and his followers. The main theme of Hegel's political philosophy is his critique of classical liberalism. Hegel argued that reason can be at home in the world only if the world is rational. Reason is manifest not only in the form of rationally acting individuals but as the essence of social and political institutions, and the highest form of reason is, he argued, expressed in the form of the modern state.

Note For modern liberals the state is a potential source of empowerment rather than of oppression.

Hegel criticised liberalism because it treats individuals in an 'atomistic form', disconnected from their social context. In liberal ideology:

- individuals are analysed exclusively as separate 'egos';
- society becomes little more that an 'aggregation' of individuals; and
- the state is simply a device for reconciling conflicting interests.

For Hegel a rational state cannot be based on the particular interests of individual egos, which threaten to develop out of control and overwhelm the state. As long as the state is regarded as nothing more than a mechanism for the defence of individual rights, liberalism will be unable to speak persuasively about such political matters as citizenship and the public good.

British followers of Hegel such as T. H. Green came to believe that classical liberalism results in a fatal split between the *private* individual and the *public* citizen. What is required is a return to 'civic virtue', which Green understood as a positive belief in the value of active citizenship and an acceptance of the need to embed individuals in coherent communities. To understand the distinction between classical and modern liberalism, the following points must be taken into consideration:

- Whereas classical liberals advocate negative freedom as freedom from coercion, modern liberals advocate a positive theory of freedom as empowerment.
- The distinction between negative and positive freedom has important implications for the role of the state in society. Classical liberals show a preference for limited state intervention (the 'minimal state'), whereas modern liberals argue that the proper function of the state is to promote 'individuality through community', by helping citizens to realise their potential.
- Classical and modern liberals hold different views on the meaning of equality. For classical liberals and libertarians, equality is understood exclusively in a formal sense. This results in a defence of **meritocracy**. Modern liberals by contrast argue that some form of distributive justice is necessary to achieve real equality of opportunity.

The limitations of Mill's definition of negative freedom were expressed by thinkers such as Green and Hobhouse, who tried to reconcile Mill's focus on the individual as the source of progress with the increasing role of the state in mass industrial society. Green redefined Mill's conception of negative freedom. According to Green, liberty entails freedom from coercion, but not just this. He maintained that the removal of constraints allowing individuals to do as they like does not in itself contribute to genuine freedom. Freedom is also bound up with defining worthwhile goals. Hence Green redefined freedom as a *positive power or capacity of doing something worth doing or enjoying*. In other words, for modern liberals liberty is defined not simply as freedom from external constraint, but freedom to do or achieve something worth-while. Green's political philosophy must be seen as part of a broader attempt to locate freedom between individuality and social responsibility. From this perspective, the state should be seen as a 'facilitator' rather than a threat to freedom:

'The state has a duty to improve people's characters and to prevent them from living unfulfilled lives, and voluntary submission to the authority of the state is indicative of the rational adjustment of individuals to those ends which they share with each other.'

As a liberal, Green did not contest the liberal belief in property rights, yet he insisted it was the responsibility of the state to regulate the unlimited accumulation of private wealth. The state should be entitled to regulate the distribution of property for purposes of freer access, but not to deprive individuals of the fruits of their labour because to do so would undermine the legal basis of the free market.

Modern liberalism thus represents a departure from **laissez faire**. Reformist liberals have sought to address problems such as urban deprivation and low educational ability. Some left-leaning liberals go further, arguing that society should be reconstructed on

communitarian lines: what is required is not an atomistic society of individuals, but a rationally organised community without extremes of wealth and poverty.

4.2 Keynes and interventionist liberalism

In the twentieth century, liberal economists such as John Maynard Keynes (1883–1946) reached the conclusion that, left unregulated, markets produce 'sub-optimal' outcomes.

According to **Keynes**, market failure occurs because there are circumstances to which the market cannot respond. For example, the market cannot take into account the social costs of economic activity, which affect society but are ignored by the businesses that produce them. Inevitably, it is governments that must act to regulate these social costs because no other agency has the capacity to do so.

Consequently, Keynes advocated state intervention to correct the problem of market failure and to balance the competing pressures of the market. During the Great Depression of the 1930s he argued that a major social cost of the market was unemployment, which the state had a duty to manage in the national interest. Although he rejected the socialist demand for a planned economy, he maintained that government should direct investment into activities such as public works in order to promote full employment. Keynes's argument that government expenditure could be used to bring an economy out of recession became economic orthodoxy in the post-war era until his ideas were challenged by the neoliberal economists in the 1970s.

4.3 Rawls and liberal equality

The most important liberal thinker in recent years was the philosopher John Rawls (1921–2002), who rejected the traditional meritocratic argument that an unequal distribution of resources in society is legitimate as long as it is based on rewarding appropriate talent. Most people in liberal capitalist societies believe that individuals deserve the fruits of their labours — that it is legitimate and proper for someone with talent to expect higher rewards for their skills. According to Rawls, this view is unacceptable not only because some individuals are born with fewer social and economic resources (and so cannot compete with the same freedom as those with greater resources), but also because we are all advantaged and/or disadvantaged by undeserved natural inequalities. It is not our fault if we are born into a poor family; neither is it our fault if we are born with few natural skills. Both are forms of undeserved injustice.

Rawls's solution was not to eliminate difference, but to organise resource allocation so that different individuals' skills and talents are harnessed for the good of the community. He offered a form of positive freedom based on a definition of what rational individuals would, in a state of complete equality, choose to do in order to minimise the potentially negative consequences of natural inequality. For Rawls, it is perfectly logical that rational individuals would wish to lessen the risks of an unequal distribution of talents by creating a just system of distribution that does not penalise undeserved natural inequality. He termed this the 'difference principle', according to which 'All social primary goods — liberty and opportunity, income and wealth, and the bases of self-respect — are to be distributed equally unless an unequal distribution of any or all of these goods is to the advantage of the least favoured.' In Rawls's liberalism the rational individual is not a self-interested **egoist**, but *someone who is able to calculate what would be best for everyone, considered impartially.* Such individuals

would logically opt to maximise their welfare were they to find themselves at the bottom of the heap.

5 *Libertarianism*

Rawls's theory of liberal equality has been criticised by libertarians not only for his use of the social-contract device, but also for his assumption that individuals entering into a contract would necessarily opt for redistributive justice. They argue that his theory of justice amounts to a defence of social democracy, and is therefore inconsistent with liberal values. **Libertarianism** is a branch of liberal thought but there are important distinctions between liberalism and libertarianism:

- Libertarians view the state as a subservient instrument of individuals rather than as an agent of society with rights over the individual.
- Libertarians who embrace evolutionary principles see them as impersonal and not subject to human modification, thus placing change and development beyond the collective direction of society; this reduces the possibility that society can be shaped into a 'rationally organised community' according to some grand design, a view which privileges the role of the autonomous individual as the primary agent of social change.

A key proponent of this tradition was the Austrian philosopher Friedrich Hayek (1899–1992), who emphasised the importance of 'naturally developing' ways of life as opposed to coercive experiments in social engineering such as communism. Hayek held an extreme faith in the autonomous individual, and in *The Road to Serfdom* attacked socialism because, in his view, it robs individuals of their autonomy, dignity and individuality. Hayek's conservative libertarianism entails a rejection of three things:

- rationalistic/deterministic ideas concerning the perfectibility of human society;
- the viability of collectivist solutions to political and economic problems; and
- abstract concepts of social justice and equality.

Hayek's libertarianism is an atomistic doctrine concerned with defending the 'moral rules of the marketplace' — an idea that was subsequently adopted by New Right theorists. Some critics have labelled his views 'anarcho–capitalist' because the only basis of legality in his scheme is respect for private property as the source of morality and social order.

Note Whereas libertarians defend the idea of the autonomous individual, anarchists advocate a *principled rejection* of all forms of organised authority.

Another key libertarian philosopher is Robert Nozick (1938–2002), who advocated the protection of negative rights (life, liberty, property) within a minimal state. He argued that only a state limited to the provision of security and enforcement of contracts can be justified, and that any state that violates individuals' rights to act in their own interests is unjustified. The consequences of this libertarian argument are twofold:

- the state cannot use coercion to force individuals to aid others (this includes the 'patterned' redistribution of resources through centrally organised mechanisms such as income tax); and
- the state cannot use coercion to prohibit individuals from engaging in certain activities, even for their own good or protection. Self-ownership is the moral right of all individuals.

6 Neoliberalism and its discontents

David Harvey, author of *A Brief History of Neoliberalism*, argues that **neoliberalism** is 'a theory of political economic practices that proposes that human wellbeing can best be advanced by liberating individual entrepreneurial freedoms and skills within an institutional framework characterised by strong private property rights, free markets, and free trade'. In addition, neoliberals link economic freedom to the pursuit of human dignity — a compelling justification, which has increased the hegemonic appeal of neoliberalism as an alternative to socialism and managed capitalism.

Neoliberalism replaced the prevailing social-democratic orthodoxy of Keynesian demand management and market regulation in the industrialised countries of the West in the 1970s and 1980s, attracting supporters around the world from Deng Xiaoping in China to General Augusto Pinochet in Chile. After the collapse of communism between 1989 and 1992, neoliberalism also won converts among reformers in Russia and Eastern Europe, whose economies are now more integrated into the global market order. Yet neoliberalism is most closely associated with Britain and the USA.

Note You should be aware of the reasons for the rise of neoliberalism in the 1970s and 1980s (see Chapter 2).

The common themes unifying all neoliberal discourse are that the state should do less and the private individual more; that the market mechanism should take precedence over artificial forms of distribution; that private ownership of the means of production is the only legitimate basis for economic organisation; that private accumulation is preferable to redistribution; and that threats to the security of private capital must be countered.

In political terms, neoliberalism appeals to governments anxious to reduce the burden of public expenditure. For example, it appeals to the libertarian New Right whose primary aim is to reverse the growing interventionist power of the state in modern society. For neoliberals, 'freedom' is understood in an exclusively *economic* sense, namely as the natural liberty of private individuals to acquire and dispose of resources without interference from public authorities.

Neoliberalism thus represents a return to the original principles of classical political economy, with one important exception: neoliberals reject protectionist policies but, unlike the early classical political economists, they do not rule out the existence of monopolistic practices. In this respect, they are distinct from radical libertarians such as Murray Rothbard (1926–95), who criticised unfair or uncompetitive commercial practices as modern-day forms of mercantilism.

In the modern global capitalist economy, financial and industrial conglomerates dominate whole sectors and, as the banking crisis of 2008–09 has shown, corporate actors are not averse to demanding government aid and market intervention when faced with bankruptcy or costly restructuring. This has led to the partial or complete nationalisation of companies and banks with unmanageable debts in order to prevent a full-blown depression. The abrupt demise of the Anglo–American model of deregulated capitalism after three decades has led many to speculate about the future: what will replace the neoliberal faith in free markets? It is difficult to answer this question, but there is some support for a return to managed capitalism. Although neoliberalism has dominated politics for three decades, it has proved to be unstable and destructive, creating inequality, uneven development and indebtedness. It has also (see Chapter 8) spawned a large anti-globalisation movement eager to resist the destructive effects of unregulated markets.

7 Civil liberties and human rights in the UK

The task of defending civil liberties and human rights in the UK falls to the judiciary. Civil liberties in the UK traditionally evolved in an unplanned, unsystematic fashion due to the absence of a codified constitution. In the Diceyan tradition, civil liberties and human rights were based on common law rather than statute law, with rulings on questions such as freedom of speech, freedom of association and freedom of the person decided in accordance with judicial precedent.

Pressure to reform the Diceyan system grew in the 1990s. Reformers demanded the introduction of a formal and codified bill of rights based on the incorporation of the European Convention on Human Rights (ECHR) into UK law. Although the UK still lacks a codified constitution, New Labour passed the ECHR into law in 1998, creating for the first time a Human Rights Act (HRA).

This new legislation, along with the abolition of the Lord Chancellor's department, the Freedom of Information Act, and the planned introduction of a new Supreme Court, has for the first time placed statutory limits on parliamentary sovereignty, providing judges with a resource to challenge the state over the correct balance between liberty and security in a democratic society. To the dismay of New Labour ministers who oversaw the introduction of the ECHR into UK law, the Law Lords have shown themselves willing to make use of the HRA to defend and reaffirm the principle of personal liberty and the right to a fair trial (*habeas corpus*) against possible violations by the state.

Although the HRA resembles a codified bill of rights similar to those in other European democracies, there are serious concerns over the increasing erosion of civil liberties and the rise of 'kneejerk illiberalism' in the UK on a number of grounds, including the extension of police powers, the expansion of routine surveillance, the use of detention without trial, and, most disturbingly, the apparent complicity of the UK intelligence services in the use of torture by the CIA in the 'war on terror'. Furthermore, as Professor Helen Fenwick argues, despite the scope of the HRA, the government can legally derogate (exempt itself) from specific clauses of the Act on the grounds of 'national security'. There is a serious risk that the freedoms specified in the HRA 'might become merely empty guarantees which cast a legitimising cloak over rights abridging legislation and executive action.'

From 2000 onwards, security legislation has been passed that is considerably more authoritarian and broad in scope than pre-HRA national security laws. These new laws include the Terrorism Act 2000, the Regulation of Investigatory Powers Act 2000, the Anti-Terrorism, Crime and Security Act 2001, the Criminal Justice Act 2003, the Prevention of Terrorism Act 2005, the Serious Organised Crime and Police Act 2005, the Terrorism Act 2006 and the Counter-Terrorism Act 2008. Of these the most controversial has been the Anti-Terrorism, Crime and Security Act 2001, which introduced the proactive measure of detention without trial. This was overruled by the Law Lords in 2004 in the Belmarsh case, which forced the Home Office to replace detention without trial with a new system of domestic control orders.

The Home Office was also defeated by the Lords in 2008 over legislation allowing police to detain suspects for 42 days without charge — a controversial policy which critics argued was incompatible with *habeas corpus*. This was followed in June 2009 by the Law Lords ruling that the use of control orders to limit the freedom of terrorist suspects without a trial based on the use of secret evidence breached human rights legislation.

In several other areas, New Labour has been criticised for allowing the creation of a 'police state' at odds with British legal and political traditions. Not only can the authorities use laws passed since 2000 to monitor 'radical' groups with no connection to terrorism (epitomised by the filming of environmental protesters by Kent Police in 2008), but there are growing fears about the rise of a surveillance culture in the UK.

How serious is this issue, and how much of a threat does it pose to civil liberties? In February 2009 a joint parliamentary committee published a report on the issue of surveillance, which criticised the tendency of the state to use 'blanket' surveillance and data accumulation. As Steven Foster, author of *The Judiciary, Civil Liberties and Human Rights*, argues, from a libertarian perspective blanket surveillance should be used only where *vital* national interests are at stake, and not for routine public-order issues.

For this reason, libertarians have opposed the Security Service Act 1996, which allows MI5 to 'assist' in criminal policing, as well as the Regulation of Investigatory Powers Act 2000, which gives the authorities greater scope to intercept private communications, e.g. e-mails and telephone calls. Finally, libertarians have also opposed Labour's plans to introduce compulsory ID cards, which, they argue, are designed not to deter criminals or terrorists but to maintain surveillance of the law-abiding majority of the population. Labour has also faced consistent opposition on this issue from the Conservatives, who argue that such projects are unnecessary and costly, and lack popular support among the electorate.

On balance, the evidence suggests that new forms of electronic/digital surveillance may be incompatible with a *liberal* democracy, in which the right to privacy is understood to be a based freedom. One of the driving forces behind the 'police state' is not the government itself but the Home Office, which exerts a strong influence over the institutional growth and development of the security apparatus. Ministers have shown themselves vulnerable to kneejerk illiberalism when confronted by demands from within the state for an extension of police and regulatory powers embodied in the legislation passed from 2000 onwards.

Key terms and concepts

Authority	The power and right to govern or issue commands
Civil society	That part of human social activity which exists outside the framework of the state, e.g. private business, the arts, media and sport
Communitarianism	Anti-liberal ideology, which emphasises the responsibility of the individual to the community and the importance of culture and established institutions
Consent	Permission to be governed, transmitted primarily through elections; in contract theory, consent provides the grounds for political obligation
Constitutionalism	Liberal belief that the powers of rulers should be subject to legal constraints

Democracy	Government by the people or their elected representatives
Egoist	Concerned for one's own interests and welfare
Enlightenment	A period of seventeenth-century European history (also known as the Age of Reason), which witnessed major advances in science and learning
Equality	Belief in the equal treatment of all individuals
Keynesianism	An economic theory associated with J. M. Keynes, who advocated the use of fiscal policy to manage demand and promote full employment
Laissez faire	Doctrine of unrestricted freedom in commerce and industry
Liberal democracy	System of government based on representative democracy and competitive elections, in which the activities of government are limited by constitutional rules or conventions
Libertarianism	Radical individualist doctrine, which holds that the state cannot use coercion to control individuals, even for their own good or protection. Self-ownership is the moral right of all individuals
Meritocracy	Rule by individuals who are chosen not because of inherited privilege but on the basis of natural talents and abilities
Neoliberalism	Economic ideology based on deregulated markets and global trade
Normativity	The application of standards and norms to guide human actions
Pluralism	The existence in a society of multiple groups with their own distinctive ethnic origins, cultural values, customs and beliefs
Political obligation	Moral and legal duty of citizens to acknowledge the authority of the state and obey the law (based on the assumption of consent)
Popular sovereignty	A system where ultimate political authority resides in the people rather than in the monarchy or the state
Rationalism	Doctrine according to which reason alone is the proper basis for determining morals and human conduct, and that knowledge can be acquired through reason without regard to experience
Rule of law	Constitutional doctrine that the ultimate source of authority in the state is the law rather than office-holders
Separation of powers	Fragmentation of government into functionally differentiated branches

CHAPTER 2 Conservatism

1 Introduction

Conservatism is a core topic in the A2 specification, and you must be able to discuss the main philosophical ideas and themes in conservative thought and relate these to historical and contemporary conservative ideologies. Of particular importance is the distinction between nineteenth-century conservatism and twentieth-century New Right ideology, in both Europe and the United States. You also need to understand the cultural determinants of conservative-type ideologies and parties, and the ways in which conservatism has adapted to new economic and political realities.

Conservatism is a feature of all societies. Conservative ideologies occupy a broad space along the political spectrum between the centre right and the far right. Conservatives share many ideas and themes, such as a respect for authority and convention, but there are major differences between **paternalistic**, libertarian and **authoritarian** forms of conservative thought, indicating the influence of cultural factors and that of alternative ideological traditions.

Conservatives traditionally stress the 'accumulated wisdom of the past', and are typically opposed to radical reform. Political conservatism emerged in the nineteenth century in reaction to the social and political upheavals of the French Revolution and the Industrial Revolution. By the mid-nineteenth century the term 'conservatism' came to denote the politics of the right. The original ideas of conservatism were formulated by thinkers such as Edmund Burke (1729–97) and Joseph de Maistre (1753–1821). They sought to preserve the authority of the monarchy and aristocracy, to maintain the social power of landowners against the emerging bourgeoisie, and to preserve the ties between church and state.

Despite continuities, modern conservatism is based on a different set of historical influences and philosophical ideas. Unlike nineteenth-century conservative thinkers, contemporary conservatives embrace capitalist modernity. Parties of the right in Europe, Asia and America remain committed to the defence of traditional values and cultural identities, but are no longer dominated by nationalist or protectionist interests.

Through a pragmatic accommodation with liberal, socialist and radical right-wing political ideas, conservatives have managed to retain political support by offering a combination of authoritarian **populism** and possessive individualism, which resonates not only among propertied interests but also among lower-middle-class and aspirational working-class voters.

Key issues and debates
- the question of human imperfection;
- the conservative preference for tradition;
- the concept of 'organic society';
- the meaning of authority in conservative ideology;
- the distinction between paternalistic and libertarian conservatism; and
- the rise of the New Right.

2 *Core ideas of conservatism*

2.1 Human imperfection

Whereas liberals argue that individuals are formed through their own autonomous will and reason, conservatives stress that human nature is flawed, demonstrating both higher and lower qualities. Liberals see the individual as a 'blank slate' without inherent qualities that impact on social life, and maintain that individuals can be improved under the right social conditions. Conservatives reject this optimistic assumption, stressing instead the 'boundedness' of human rationality, and the importance of culture and identity in politics.

In the conservative world-view, humans have a capacity for reason but more fundamentally are security-seeking creatures, dependent and morally corruptible. Although this scepticism is less marked in libertarian New Right conservatism, the view that human nature is fallible is reflected in the conservative preference for institutions and structures that promote normative guidance (authority) and social stability.

Conservatives thus advocate a *pragmatic* approach to politics. For philosophers such as Professor Michael Oakeshott (1901–90), politics is a potentially boundless enterprise, and human beings need a firm 'moral compass' if they are to avoid 'drifting at sea' or succumbing to complexity and uncertainty. **Pragmatism** and experience, rather than 'doctrinal simplicity', are essential, just as firm normative principles are necessary for guiding human conduct.

2.2 Tradition

Tradition refers to the beliefs, institutions, customs and practices handed down from one generation to the next. All societies possess traditions, which are viewed as essential to the self-image of the group. Conservatives emphasise the importance of national traditions and identity, particularly in relation to other cultures. They emphasise tradition for two reasons:

- Tradition represents the 'accumulated wisdom of the past'. If an institution or custom has stood the test of time, then it is inherently worth preserving. In this respect, Edmund Burke maintained that 'change is only necessary in order to conserve'. Whereas liberals advocate reform, conservatives seek to *legitimise the present in terms of the past*. The institution of monarchy, for example, is a symbolic part of a nation's history. This institution has survived in some countries despite centuries of political upheaval and change, and therefore deserves to be defended.
- Tradition also strengthens social integration through the maintenance of a common past and a common identity. This is necessary to promote what conservatives term 'connectedness', namely the sense that people have of belonging in a specific place and time. Traditions and social institutions evolve 'organically' and cannot be manufactured or transferred arbitrarily from one society to another without losing their unique and essential quality.

However, the idea that conservatism is based exclusively on *opposition* to social and political change is misleading. It is important to acknowledge that conservatives can be either traditional or radical in their attitude to change, a fact that becomes clear when we examine the differences between paternalistic and libertarian forms of conservative thought.

2.3 Hierarchy and authority

Conservatives argue that leadership and authority are essential features of social organisation. There is an intuitive assumption among conservative thinkers that human wellbeing can best be achieved in communities subject to political authority. Authority is understood as a vital resource for the maintenance of stable and prosperous communities. Authority augments, or adds to, the power of superiors by encouraging citizens to believe that their commands are both rightful and legitimate. Without this belief in authority, societies lack integration and social order becomes more difficult to sustain without resort to coercion.

The functional importance of authority in conservatism can be summarised as follows:
- authority provides normative guidance;
- authority simplifies decision-making;
- authority reduces complexity; and
- authority promotes cooperation and social order.

Conservatives defend authority because they believe that, without adequate guidance and instruction from authority figures, law and order dissolve. This is a central theme in the neoconservative critique of left-wing radicalism, which right-wing political theorists blame for the rise of delinquency in late modern societies. Respect for **hierarchy** and authority is also understood as an obligation, a means for individuals to give something back to the community of which they are a part.

For conservatives, authority is embodied in social and political institutions. The most important of these are:
- the state (political authority is a distinctive resource, based on popular recognition of the justified character of government);
- the armed forces (as institutions providing security, the military and police are understood to be essential to the defence of public order);
- the legal system (judges and lawyers determine the legality or illegality of actions, defending the rule of law);
- education (teachers promote discipline, hard work and achievement, providing role models for young people);
- religion (religious leaders embody moral authority); and
- the family (the traditional family is the basic unit of social organisation and primary socialisation).

Authoritarian conservatives portray authority as *absolute and unquestionable*, and oppose constitutionalism as an unnecessary constraint on their authority to govern. However, libertarian and paternalistic conservatives tend to agree that there must be boundaries to authority and constraints on office-holders: excessive authority risks creating a repressive, militaristic society.

2.4 Organic society

The idea that society develops organically is a key theme in conservative ideology, but has been challenged by New Right theorists. The metaphor of a biological organism is used to demonstrate the idea of 'interdependence', as well as the necessary 'obligation' of individuals to the community:

- *Traditional* conservatives reject the atomistic perspective of liberalism, which views society as an 'aggregation of individuals'. Adopting a 'communitarian' perspective, traditional conservatives see individualism as both ontologically and motivationally false: ontologically because not all the properties of groups can be reduced to individuals, i.e. the total is greater than the sum of its parts; motivationally because there are cases when people cooperate and depend on one another for mutual benefit rather than simply to obtain private goods.
- *Libertarian New Right* conservatives, by contrast, adopt an individualist view of society. Although they defend the idea of social order, duty and moral obligation, these concepts are understood primarily in terms of individual self-reliance and private property. New Right theorists stress the idea of 'ordered risk-taking' within a secure economic and political environment, and assert the moral primacy of individuals and families over society as a whole.

Note The branch of philosophy known as 'ontology' is concerned with *what there is in the world*, i.e. what exists.

The idea of society as a fragile **organic** entity finds greater expression in continental-European conservatism than in Britain. This is particularly the case in France and Germany, where reactionary conservatism has a long and established tradition.

In Britain, the organic-society metaphor is embodied in the paternalistic ethos of 'faith, family and nation' as vital parts of the moral fabric of society. As Professor Noël O'Sullivan argues, this conception of organic unity has gradually given way to a more pragmatic vision of a *balanced constitution* and *broad social consensus*.

In France the ideal of the organic society has traditionally found expression in the emphasis on order, spiritual duty and honour as antidotes to the perceived moral and cultural decline of modern society and the weakness of mass democracy. In Germany the ideal of society as an organic entity has been a feature of romantic conservatism since the early nineteenth century. German conservatism has been marked by a strongly corporatist tendency, as well as hostility towards modern industrial civilisation and the abstract ideals of the Enlightenment.

2.5 Property

Conservatives, like liberals, attach particular importance to the institution of private property, and for obvious reasons conservative parties have traditionally found their bedrock of support among the propertied classes. However, whereas liberals maintain that private property symbolises rights in a concrete form, for conservatives property assumes a more profound significance as a guarantor of social order, privilege and personal identity.

- Private property is indicative of the individual's 'stake' in society. According to this view, the property owner has an interest in social order, a natural tendency to obey the law and an obligation to respect the private property of others.
- Property should be seen as a legitimate reward for individuals' natural talents and energies. Individuals should be allowed to enjoy the fruits of their own labour, and the acquisition of material wealth functions as a powerful incentive for industriousness.

- Property provides people with security in an uncertain world. For example, home ownership provides security of tenure, while personal wealth reduces the probability that the individual will become dependent on state welfare.
- Finally, property provides people with an opportunity to express their individuality. *Choice* is a key factor in the rise of consumer culture, which functions by encouraging individuals to differentiate themselves through their material possessions.

3 Conservatism: ideology or disposition?

A long-standing debate in political theory concerns the status of conservatism as an 'ideology' or a 'disposition'. Those who see conservatism as a disposition maintain that conservatives are by nature opposed to abstract or theoretical ideas. They associate *ideology* with doctrinaire groups such as Marxists, anarchists and feminists, who advocate a radical, sectarian view of the world and how it should be organised. From this perspective, 'ideology' is understood in a pejorative sense. By contrast, conservatism is a *habit of mind*, a common-sense world-view suggesting that rationality lies not in dreaming up grand schemes or experiments in social engineering, but in a gradualist approach to reform. What defines conservatism is not what it stands for *as such*, but its hostility towards radical ideas and its defence of *existing* ways of life.

On the other hand, some theorists view conservatism as a political ideology like any other. From a Marxist perspective, paternalistic conservatism is a ruling-class ideology based on the idea that the ruling class claims a right and a duty to govern by virtue of its superior birth and status. Conservatism legitimises the power of ruling elites by ascribing to them superior competence in the activity of government.

From this perspective, populist New Right conservatism is simply an adjustment of the traditional ruling formula, an attempt to broaden the legitimacy of the capitalist system by extending incentives such as home ownership, social mobility and personal consumption to a broader constituency.

Conservatism cannot be equated exclusively with a defence of the status quo for the following reasons:

- Conservatives uphold tradition, but tradition *itself* is typically an expression of socially and historically embedded interests. Traditional customs and institutions can be seen as concrete manifestations of the aspirations and social power of different groups, and by defending certain traditions, e.g. respect for private property and defence of the nuclear family, conservatism attempts to legitimate social practices at an ideological level.
- Conservatives have often adopted radical positions, e.g. extending the franchise in the Representation of the People Act 1867. It is often argued that Benjamin Disraeli (1804–81) took this initiative for pragmatic reasons (to increase support for the Conservative Party among the urban propertied classes). Yet this crucial reform ultimately paved the way for the introduction of a universal franchise in 1918 (1928 for women), which has had far-reaching consequences for the nature of representative democracy in Britain.
- Conservatism is not purely reactive. While traditionalists may be concerned with defending the status quo, conservatives stand for ideas and values in a positive sense. This can be seen in the case of public-sector reform in the UK in the 1980s, a policy subsequently adopted by liberal and social democratic parties in Britain and elsewhere in Europe.

- Conservatism comprises a *plurality* of different viewpoints, some more radical, some more moderate. Like all political ideologies, conservatism has both extremist and moderate supporters. In this respect, the differences between liberal conservatives in Britain and right-wing **neoconservatives** in the USA could not be greater.

4 *Paternalistic conservatism*

The ideology of paternalistic conservatism has a long history in the UK, but also has deep roots in other European countries. In Britain, this tradition can be traced back to 'One Nation Conservatism'. In Germany, Italy and other continental-European countries, it is usually referred to as **Christian democracy**. In its simplest sense, paternalistic conservatism is based on the idea that government should *provide for and regulate the lives of its citizens as a father does for his children*.

Paternalistic conservatives thus assume a kind of 'benevolent **elitism**', which holds that the ruling class is 'born to rule' as a result of superior status and education. However, in so doing the ruling class also has a duty to promote the welfare of the people.

'One Nation' conservative ideology is associated with Disraeli, who stated that the greatest threat to social order lay in the failure to integrate the poorer classes into mainstream society. As Professor Robert Eccleshall argues, paternalistic conservatism offers a vision of the community as an organic unity 'bound by a hierarchy of privileges and obligations in which wealth is held in trust for the common benefit, and where in consequence those with power have a responsibility to attend to the welfare of the mass of the people.'

The paternalistic conservative view that welfare is a responsibility of the privileged classes inspired the passage of humanitarian legislation in the late nineteenth century, and Disraeli exemplified the belief that moderate reform is essential to preserve the foundations of the established order. He argued that:

'In a progressive country change is constant; and the great question is not whether you should resist change which is inevitable, but whether that change should be carried out in deference to the manners, the customs, the laws, and the traditions of the people, or... in deference to abstract principles, and arbitrary and general doctrines.'

This tendency persisted into the twentieth century and remains a feature of middle-of-the-road British conservatism to the present day. Tory party leaders such as Harold Macmillan (1894–1986) and Winston Churchill (1874–1965) typify the 'One Nation' world-view, which led the British Conservative Party to tolerate and adapt to the post-war social-democratic consensus as a necessary — if perhaps regrettable — feature of managed welfare capitalism. Key features of this social-democratic consensus include:
- mixed economy (private and state ownership);
- redistributive taxation;
- social welfare;
- state-funded education and health care;
- state pension schemes;
- negotiated withdrawal from empire; and
- European integration.

A similar outlook underlies the European tradition of Christian democracy, particularly in West Germany after the Second World War. This ideological tradition, represented most famously by Konrad Adenauer (1876–1967), has its roots in political Catholicism and the Centre Party of the Weimar era. The key features of this tradition can be summarised as follows:

- Like traditional conservatives in Britain, Christian democrats argue that the state has a duty to regulate the negative social consequence of the free market. Christian democrats believe in a 'social-market economy' rather than a 'free-market economy'.
- Christian democrats advocate a defence of civil society through the promotion of non-state social entities, such as trade unions, family organisations and church-based associations.
- Christian democrats attempt to transcend traditional class-based allegiances by advocating a neo-communitarian ideology of the 'common good'.

5   Libertarian conservatism

If paternalistic conservatism is based on a communitarian perspective, libertarian conservatism represents an altogether different approach. In contrast to paternalists, libertarian conservatives advocate an explicitly ideological rejection of the social democratic consensus outlined above. The primary aim of libertarian conservatives is to *liberate the economy from political regulation.*

Libertarian conservatism is based on a set of core assumptions about human economic life and the correct limits of state intervention in the economy. As will be clear from the previous chapter, libertarians such as Friedrich Hayek privilege the role of autonomous individuals as the primary agents of social change, and reject attempts to achieve an organised, collective direction of human affairs. Hayek believed in spontaneous development, but also believed that social order is possible based on a self-organising system of voluntary cooperation.

At the heart of libertarian conservatism is a commitment to the market based on the *natural inequality* of individuals. For the libertarian New Right, the one-sided defence of social stability is inconsistent not only with economic freedom, but also with the basic features of human nature. New Right ideology is concerned less with the preservation of culture than with adaptation to the rationality of the market:

> Whereas traditionalists see society as a hierarchy of privileges and obligations, libertarians view the cultural and institutional fabric of society as the context within which individuals interact for their *own individual advantage.*

In this sense libertarian conservatives dismiss the communitarian emphasis of paternalist conservatism in favour of *bourgeois individualism.* The principal elements of this libertarian agenda can be summarised as follows:

- Universal acceptance of the rules of the free market.
- State intervention and government planning reduced to a minimum.
- The welfare state gradually abolished.

It would be a mistake, however, to assume that this overtly anti-collectivist agenda detracts from the conservative character of libertarian conservatism. This is because libertarian conservatives set out to reverse what they see as the negative consequences of social democracy for *conservative* reasons — namely to increase self-reliance, industriousness and personal responsibility, to reduce the extent of state intervention in the private sphere of individuals, and to reassert traditional forms of authority. It is these concerns that motivate libertarian conservatives, who champion the *moral rules of the market* as a basis for a property-owning democracy in which the scope of politics is reduced to the provision of security, reversing the collective regulation and decision-making that characterise social-democratic political systems.

6 *Authoritarian conservatism*

Authoritarian conservatism is a *reactionary* ideology that has traditionally flourished in southern and eastern European countries, as well as in Latin America, Asia and the Middle East. Advocates of political authoritarianism in the nineteenth century stressed the need to conserve the traditional structures and institutions of society in the transition to modernity. Writers such as Burke and De Maistre emphasised the importance of preserving existing structures and ways of life by means of authoritarian *rule from above*.

Modern-day authoritarian conservative regimes employ repressive measures to *restrict the growth of pluralism and democracy in the path towards social and economic modernisation*. Such regimes exhibit a political outlook that favours obedience to authority rather than personal liberty and individualism, and that seeks to maintain the social influence of traditional institutions such as the military and the Church. The main features of authoritarian conservatism are:

- Suppression of democracy (authoritarian conservatives mistrust popular sovereignty, preferring rule from above, or at least restricted democracy).
- Oligarchy (rule by the few) — political decisions should be made by elites who understand the realities of politics.
- Anti-pluralism (excessive party-political competition and ideological polarisation undermine political stability).
- Anti-communism (authoritarian conservatives are by definition opposed to social equality).
- Defence of traditional values (authoritarian conservatives defend **patriarchy**, hierarchy and nationalism).
- Militarism (martial values should play a greater role in civil society, e.g. in the education system).
- **Clericalism** (authoritarian conservatives defend organised religion against modern, secular ideals and in some cases against scientific rationality).

Three examples of authoritarian conservatism are:

- The Greek Colonels' regime (1967–74), which suspended democratic institutions, outlawed political parties and suppressed all left-wing organisations. The regime also introduced a reactionary social policy aimed at reasserting traditional values and customs, patriarchy and the authority of the Orthodox Church.
- The regime of Augusto Pinochet in Chile (1973–88), which ousted the Marxist government of Salvador Allende in a *coup d'état*. Pinochet's government combined neoliberal economic policies with an authoritarian political agenda aimed at restricting the development of pluralism, democracy and civil rights in Chilean society.
- The Islamic Republic of Iran, created in 1979, which is led by a theocratic religious caste supported by the military and parties of the right. Although formally democratic, the Iranian regime is both anti-liberal and anti-pluralist, and cultivates anti-Westernism to bolster its political support.

Note You should be careful not to confuse authoritarian conservatism with fascism. Authoritarian conservatism *suppresses* political activity while fascism promotes a *politicisation of everyday life* by mobilising society behind nationalist goals.

7 The New Right

The New Right emerged in the 1970s in response to the crisis of hegemony in the social-democratic systems of the West. The origins of the New Right are in some respects contradictory, given the disparity between its *neoliberal* and *neoconservative* currents. Yet the neoliberal and neoconservative critiques of 'big government' share an ideological premise, namely to challenge egalitarianism and reduce the expectations of what governments can and should do in the name of citizens.

For Professor Andrew Gamble, New Right conservatism entails a belief in the *free economy and the strong state*. The logic of this formula rests on the assumption that the use of coercive state power can be justified as a means for defeating and containing interests that threaten the operation of the free-market economy. 'If the state makes the protection of those institutions of the free economy its priority,' he argues, 'then it creates the basis of its own legitimacy.'

An authoritarian state is necessary for the following reasons:

- to reduce the size of the public sector and the extent of state intervention;
- to police the new market order;
- to increase the efficiency of the economy; and
- to reassert traditional forms of social and political authority.

However, while there is a compatibility between neoliberal and neoconservative views on the purpose and extent of government, there are tensions between these ideological currents. On the one hand, **neoliberalism** entails a commitment to liberty, individualism and freedom of choice. On the other hand, neoconservatism promotes an authoritarian conception of law and order that is inconsistent with libertarian ideas of personal freedom.

7.1 Neoliberalism

In the post-war years traditional paternalistic conservatives had favoured accommodation with the institutions of welfarist social democracy. With the end of the post-war boom in America and Europe, this ideological accommodation was rejected by exponents of the New Right who argued that middle-way conservatism was effectively an appeasement of socialism. New Right ideologists sought instead to reassert the hegemony of the liberal–capitalist system by rolling back the frontiers of the state, by strengthening the institutions of finance capital, and in the UK by attempting to address the long-term problem of 'managed decline'. The emphasis of neoliberalism can be broken down into four main ideas:

- *Defence of individual economic freedom*. Returning to the original ideas of classical political economy, neoliberals emphasise the idea of individuals as rational utility-maximisers. Choices about resource allocation and consumption should be up to individuals themselves, who are best qualified to make decisions about their own welfare.
- *Reduction of state intervention*. Neoliberals advocate a shift away from Keynesian fiscal and monetary policies, and focus instead on inflation. Whereas post-war governments sought to maintain full employment, neoliberals argued that this was not possible without negative consequences for the economy as a whole. Governments

should refrain from using fiscal instruments such as taxation to promote social ends, and should reverse the culture of rising expectations of state intervention.

- *Deregulation.* Neoliberals stress the need for *unrestricted private commerce* in place of state management and planning. They argue that excessive state regulation and the growth of the public sector undermine the competitiveness and efficiency of economies, and they advocate the deregulation of business and finance, a return to market forces and reduced corporate taxation as the best means for generating and sustaining an enterprise culture.

Note The controversy over deregulation following the banking crisis of 2008–09 demonstrates the limits of this economic theory. Critics of neoliberalism argue that state regulation is essential to mitigate risk.

- *Anti-welfarism.* Neoliberals favour a reduction in the total cost of welfare as a proportion of national income. They argue that paternalism leads to welfare dependency and a decline in self-reliance, as a result of which individuals lose the incentive to work and provide for themselves. Welfarism is viewed as an unintended outcome of well-meaning social democratic policies that have debilitating consequences for individual liberty and human self-worth.

7.2 Neoconservatism

Neoconservatism emerged in the USA as a reaction against 'big government' and left-wing radicalism. In its original form, however, neoconservatism was not a typical example of right-wing political reaction. Rather, it grew out of the disillusionment of Cold War liberals with the appeasement of the USSR during the period of détente (1973–80), and the leftward radicalisation of the Democrats during the McGovern/ Carter era. Neoconservatism is associated with a group of Jewish-American intellectuals, whose principal representatives include Irving Kristol, Norman Podhoretz and Daniel Bell. These thinkers acquired the label 'neoconservative' as a result of their hostility towards the New Left, but were unable to influence mainstream politics until a group of Washington insiders with links to the Hudson Institute and the Project for the New American Century joined the Republican Party in the 1990s.

In a foreign-political sense, neoconservatives combine a right-wing belief in military force with an internationalist defence of liberal democracy against all forms of *totalitarianism*. In a domestic sense, however, neoconservatives are typically opposed to egalitarian programmes and campaigns designed to help underprivileged groups obtain fairer access to primary goods such as liberty and opportunity, income and wealth. We can summarise their main ideological concerns as follows:

- *Opposition to 'big government'.* Like neoliberals, neoconservatives oppose welfare as a misguided outcome of well-meaning liberal/social-democratic policies. A key theme in neoconservatism is the concept of *ungovernability*. According to theorists such as Daniel Bell and Seymour Martin Lipset, the more the state attempts to do, the more it risks being overwhelmed by the growth of excessive expectations. This has encouraged neoconservatives to focus instead on national-security and foreign-policy issues.
- *Defence of natural inequality.* For neoconservatives liberty depends on the ability of *sovereign individuals* to pursue their economic goals unaided and unhindered by the state. Liberty is understood not in an abstract universal sense, but in

traditional patriarchal terms as households represented by male breadwinners. Neoconservatives believe that social inequality is a natural feature of the division of labour in market societies, and is thus outside the legitimate scope of government action.

- *Anti-permissive society*. Combined with this assault on welfarism, neoconservatives advocate a traditionalist social agenda, which highlights the moral bankruptcy of 'permissive' societies. For neoconservatives, there is a contradiction between the rationalisation of modern society and the permissive modernist culture (which undermines the very basis of a rationally organised society by generating subversion and a crisis of authority). Neoconservatives thus advocate a return to traditional virtues such as self-reliance, religious observance and 'family values', without which, they argue, society is in danger of becoming decadent, hedonistic and corrupt. It is only through regeneration — through the *normalising power of tradition* — that Western societies can possibly hope to reclaim their moral foundation.

> **Note** Not all New Right conservatives necessarily support all of these principles with equal enthusiasm. Libertarians are wary of preaching, and identify with neoconservatism only to the extent that it promotes economic freedom.

At the heart of neoconservatism is a belief in the family as the primary institution of social reproduction and social order. Although the family as a source of social and moral solidarity has been weakened by the impact of the free market (increased atomism, individualism and social mobility have led to the breakdown of extended families and the entry of women into the workforce), the neoconservative focus on family values aims to bolster the traditional nuclear family. For neoconservatives, social order is dependent on the following attributes:

- parental discipline;
- paternal responsibility;
- patriarchal authority;
- anti-feminism;
- heterosexual marriage;
- **patriotism** and national identity; and
- religious observance.

Although there is a compatibility between market libertarians and neoconservatives in relation to the role of the state, there are potential contradictions between these two currents of thought:

- Unrestricted economic freedom exacerbates social problems such as unemployment and social inequality, which undermine social stability. This paradoxically increases the need for state intervention, e.g. welfare benefits and law and order, to manage the social pressures of the free market.
- New Right theorists criticise the tendency towards cultural decadence and permissiveness, but fail to acknowledge that a key source of this problem is the *consumer culture* created by capitalism, which promotes materialism and an unlimited choice of lifestyle options, many of which are disapproved of by neoconservatives.
- The demand for an authoritarian state has negative implications for civil liberties. In the past two decades, governments committed to *liberal* economic policies have introduced *illiberal* legislation that restricts the rights of individuals to engage in activities that may threaten the secure operation of the free market.

An example of this contradiction between freedom and stability is the impact of market forces on society. Market forces increase social mobility and uproot communities, causing dislocation and rapid change. Whereas earlier generations could expect less change, with a single job for life, economic rationalisation means it is harder for families to plan for the future and create a stable environment for children. Although New Right thinkers are anti-feminist (celebrating the ideal of the devoted mother), the reality of the labour market means that it is increasingly necessary for most women to work so that families can make ends meet.

8 The development of conservatism in the UK

In the late 1960s and early 1970s, senior Conservatives in the UK such as Enoch Powell, Keith Joseph and Margaret Thatcher began a process that ultimately led to the realignment of British politics. Powell, in particular, identified two key issues facing British policymakers: first, the need to redefine Britain's place in the world following the retreat from empire; second, the need to stem the growth of state intervention in the economy.

Like Powell, Thatcher reasserted the importance of economic freedom within the framework of a cohesive, ordered nation-state. 'Thatcherism' fused neoliberalism and neoconservatism in an authoritarian–populist strategy in which the legitimacy of the state was linked to the defence of a free market. Here we can see the logic of New Right ideology in practice, namely using the power of the state to determine once and for all *the proper limits* of state intervention.

8.1 Market libertarianism

The best example of market libertarianism is the *privatisation* of state monopolies. This was aimed at addressing the problem of 'failing' public-sector companies, either by introducing market forces or by selling off the industry to the private sector in order to attract investment. During the 1980s, all but a handful of the UK's nationalised concerns were sold off below their market value. This stimulated financial activity in the City, promoting share ownership among the middle classes, which in turn allowed the Conservatives to depict themselves as a party committed to creating *property-owning democracy*.

Another example of market libertarianism is *deregulation*. Deregulation refers primarily to the reduction of constraints on the free operation of markets, e.g. the deregulation of the London stock market in the mid-1980s. Although this has created problems for the banks (which acquired too many bad debts, leading to the failure of the banking system in 2008), deregulation in the 1980s and 1990s encouraged individuals with modest means to invest in shares by reducing transaction costs and providing tax incentives.

The most successful policy of the Conservatives in the 1980s was privatisation, notably the 'right-to-buy' scheme. This was a populist attempt to promote home ownership among lower-middle-class voters and affluent workers. This policy followed logically from the idea of share ownership, and was designed to generate broader public acceptance of free-enterprise capitalism among former Labour voters. It was also designed to increase consumerism and popular identification with capitalism.

8.2 Authoritarian populism

For New Right conservatives in the UK, economic freedom is contingent on the freedom of 'sovereign individuals of capitalism' to acquire and exchange resources. Hall and Jacques, editors of *The Politics of Thatcherism*, coined the term 'authoritarian

populism' to describe the political character of the New Right thinking in Britain. Although Britain is not an authoritarian society as such, the appeal of authoritarian populism is linked to the idea that populist economic policies based on free enterprise and a defence of private property are compatible with a traditional conservative emphasis on authority, personal responsibility, law and order and discipline.

The New Right emphasis on law and order has assumed many forms, but was originally designed to counter the 'ungovernability crisis' of the British state. Leading neoconservative thinkers believed that *increasing* expectations of state intervention and *decreasing* respect for traditional institutions and values had resulted in a crisis of legitimacy in the state. The Tories argued that this ungovernability crisis could be addressed only by neutralising social movements and sectional interests that placed excessive demands on the state. For this reason, Margaret Thatcher targeted left-wing trade unions, such as the National Union of Mineworkers, that had previously challenged the elected authority of the government.

This resulted in practice in a divisive 'two-nation' strategy based on a class-specific defence of social respectability. Whereas Tory paternalists had traditionally defended the One Nation ideal as a means of integrating middle-class and lower-middle-class voters behind the goals of the Establishment, in Thatcherism two nations can be identified:

- a hegemonic nation of respectable middle-class citizens in employment ('our people');
- a subordinate nation of non-skilled workers, non-British minorities, the unemployed and the socially excluded.

The result was increased social inequality and polarisation, which exploded in 1990 in a popular revolt against the community charge ('poll tax'), a neoconservative policy initiative that prefigured Thatcher's own fall from power.

9 *Conservatism after Thatcher*

9.1 The impact of the New Right

The impact of the New Right was profound. For nearly three decades, neoliberalism became the central component of the new consensus politics — a hegemonic ideology that heralded the rise of globalisation and the new world order. Although many voters in the UK rejected Thatcher's authoritarianism, there is little doubt that her emphasis on private enterprise, self-sufficiency and deregulation — and the authoritarian–populist defence of law and order — struck a chord with the British electorate.

Professor Ruth Levitas argues that opposition to a hegemonic ideology should not be taken as evidence of its failure. 'Hegemony does not require that *all of the people* are convinced *all of the time*,' she says. 'A dominant ideology is dominant not just by its receipt of a majority vote, but because it is propagated and supported by the institutions of civil society and the state. Hegemony simply requires a degree of assent, which it is well-placed to elicit; but more importantly it must prevent the emergence of coherent counter-ideologies.'

The hegemony of the New Right can also be measured by the transformation of the Labour Party under Tony Blair as Labour leaders adjusted to new political realities. This is illustrated by Gordon Brown's decision as chancellor to allow the Bank of England control over monetary policy (interest rates), thereby reducing the power of the state to intervene in the economy for political reasons. Labour has also used 'stealth taxes' and national-insurance contributions to finance increased public spending in the knowledge that the electorate will punish any party that increases income tax.

On the other hand, it is clear that Thatcherism was the outcome of a unique constellation of historical and political factors. Political observers argue that the hegemonic strategy of the New Right in the 1980s was an inherently unstable mixture of economic and political ideas that did not survive Thatcher's departure from Downing Street in 1990. In this respect, David Marsh and R. A. W. Rhodes, editors of *Implementing Thatcherite Policies*, suggest that the focus on Thatcherism as an ideological movement exaggerates its actual impact on British politics. They point to the constraints on even the most energetic reformist leaders: even leaders with a 'personalised mandate' are subject to the constraints of office and can only achieve a small proportion of their goals. Three aspects of New Right policy proved to be unsuccessful:

- *The attempt to abolish the welfare state*. A key aspect of Conservative policy in the 1980s was the attempt to reverse the trend towards increasing expenditure on welfare. Although efforts were made to reign in the public sector, the welfare state remains and government expenditure continues to rise as a percentage of GDP. Thatcherism certainly challenged the very institutions of the welfare system, but fell short of abolishing the system of taxation and redistribution that guarantees the survival of the NHS and the social-security system.
- *The attempt to create a new moral majority based on neoconservative social values*. Although the 'Victorian values' campaign can be seen as a successful example of neoconservative ideology put into practice, the 'moral majority' failed to catch on in the UK as it did in the United States. As the journalist Beatrix Campbell argues, the crusade of the moral majority in the UK failed because it did not offer female voters an alternative to the practical realities of career/motherhood that have characterised the experience of British women in the workforce since 1945. Although John Major tried to appeal to the moral majority with his 'Back to Basics' campaign, this ill-fated policy was abandoned in the wake of repeated accusations of government corruption and sex scandals.
- *The attempt to prevent the increasing integration of the UK into the European Union*. The New Right failed to achieve its core goal of renegotiating Britain's membership of the EU. Despite the emergence of the UK Independence Party, most voters recognise the benefits of EU membership. The Conservatives have ruled out joining the single currency, but there has been no return to the more virulent anti-European rhetoric of the 1980s and early 1990s.

9.2 Ideological developments since 1997

The Conservatives lost the 1997 election for four main reasons:

(i)   the recession of the early 1990s;
(ii) the split over Europe;
(iii) the public perception of sleaze; and
(iv) the 'Blair effect'.

The ideological crisis of the Tories after 1997 can be seen most clearly in the attempt by William Hague to adjust to the new realities of the Blair era. Following New Labour's landslide victory, Hague vacillated between a libertarian form of conservatism and a revised form of authoritarian populism. It is possible to identify two distinct versions of conservative ideology under Hague's leadership:

- *Hague 'Mark I'*. Hague's first attempt to set a new agenda for the Right entailed an attack on New Labour's intrusive communitarianism and 'political correctness'. As Richard Kelly, author of *Changing Party Policy in Britain*, argues, Hague, in an effort to resuscitate a version of libertarian Toryism, tried to adapt the Conservative emphasis on economic freedom to the area of social policy. Portraying himself as an advocate of personal freedom, Hague argued that, just as the state has no right to intervene in the *economic* activities of citizens, so it has no right to tell people how they should live their lives. Yet the problem with this ideological strategy was clear: if the party abandoned its traditional conservative defence of authority, then what did it really stand for? How could it differentiate itself from the other main parties if it abandoned this crucial part of its identity?

- *Hague 'Mark II'*. Hague realised that his lurch towards libertarianism was unpopular with the Tory faithful and made little impact with the electorate. As a result, he made a radical U-turn back towards what he termed (rather unfortunately) 'common-sense conservatism'. This new brand of Conservative ideology was based on a reassertion of the power of the state to defend law and order, the 'British way of life' and the primacy of heterosexual marriage, as well as a host of traditional 'boot-and-braces' values, e.g. hard work, discipline and self-reliance. This U-turn failed to achieve its desired objective, and was widely seen as out of touch with the changing multi-ethnic, multi-faith and tolerant character of British society. Although Hague's attack on asylum-seekers, illegal immigrants and welfare fraudsters resonated with the right-wing tabloids, it registered little support outside the party faithful and served to alienate younger voters from what was increasingly seen as the 'nasty party'.

Following Hague's resignation, the 'fatal dilemma' of British conservatism was again brought into focus by the confrontation between libertarians, who backed Michael Portillo and Ken Clarke, and authoritarians who favoured the candidate of the Right, Iain Duncan Smith. After winning the leadership election Duncan Smith accepted the advice of the party's chairwoman, Theresa May, that the Tories needed to get away from their image as the 'nasty party', but his lack of charisma, coupled with the then unprecedented level of satisfaction with New Labour, undermined all attempts to develop an effective political strategy.

In an attempt to differentiate the party from New Labour, the conservatives have adopted a set of policies that rehearse some of the key themes of the New Right. Since David Cameron won the leadership contest in 2005, the emphasis of the party's strategy has been to oppose New Labour's profligate spending on the public sector. Demonstrating the continuing importance of the party's Thatcherite legacy, the Conservatives argue that schools, hospitals and other key services function best if they are taken out of state control.

David Cameron can be seen as a *pragmatic* conservative for whom ideology and policy are less important than presentation and leadership style. But he has been consistent in his opposition to New Labour's more authoritarian instincts, e.g. in the campaign against ID cards. This reflects not just the libertarian credentials of the current leadership, but also the widespread unpopularity of 'surveillance culture' among British voters.

The Conservatives have also been trying to reposition themselves as the party of 'economic competence'. Although they acknowledge the political importance of the welfare state and the NHS (exemplified by Cameron's public affirmation of the need for an efficient health service), the party remains committed to marketisation, decentralisation and private-sector competition as an alternative to Labour's policy of increased spending on education and the NHS.

The main elements of current Conservative Party policy include:
- increased marketisation and decentralisation of education and the health service;
- reduced income tax (to be funded through reduced public spending);
- reduction of 'stealth taxes';
- decreased regulation of businesses;
- increasing restrictions on immigration and political asylum;
- opposition to the European single currency;
- opposition to the EU Constitution;
- bipartisan support for the so-called 'war on terror' (including the Iraq war);
- support for rural interests, e.g. the Countryside Alliance; and
- opposition to aspects of New Labour's security and anti-terrorism legislation.

The continued defence of market libertarianism and national sovereignty represents basic continuity with the party's Thatcherite legacy. Although Conservatives still defend traditional institutions and values, the party has shown little appetite for a return to the paternalistic Toryism of the pre-Thatcher era. In this respect, the ideological emphasis of the party is biased towards a defence of the free market rather than towards social stability and social cohesion, which has made it more difficult for the Conservatives to offer a coherent alternative to New Labour's partial nationalisation of the banking system.

Key terms and concepts

Authoritarianism	Political outlook that favours obedience to authority rather than liberty
Christian democracy	Paternalistic conservative ideology in Western and central Europe that accepts the need for a social-market economy
Clericalism	Support for the traditional authority of the Church in society
Elitism	Political doctrine that advocates rule by social and political elites
Hierarchy	Form of social organisation in which individuals are ranked according to authority or dominance
Neoconservatism	Reformulation of conservative doctrine emphasising the importance of family values, tradition, national defence and the free market
Neoliberalism	Economic ideology based on deregulated markets and global trade
Organicism	Traditional conservative doctrine that advocates an 'organic' metaphor of society as an integrated, living entity with deep roots in the past
Paternalism	The principle and practice of paternal administration; the belief that government must supply the needs and regulate the lives of citizens as a father does his children
Patriarchy	Male domination in politics and society (see Chapter 7)
Patriotism	Pride in and attachment to the traditions and culture of one's country
Populism	Style of politics that aims to maximise the popularity of government by introducing policies with a mass appeal (e.g. tax cuts)
Pragmatism	World-view that emphasises common-sense judgement and everyday human experience in preference to abstract theory
Tradition	An established custom or practice (specific to nations/cultures)

1 Introduction

Whereas liberalism is associated with the rise of the bourgeoisie, socialism is linked to the rise of the industrial working class in the late nineteenth and early twentieth centuries. Socialism is concerned with a critique of the present (the political–economic conditions of society as it exists) and a projected idealisation of the future (how an ideal society might look). This involves a leap of faith and imagination, an emotional as well as intellectual commitment to the view that something that has never existed — equality — is nonetheless both normal and possible.

Socialism can be understood as an attempt to achieve the goals of liberalism without accepting the inevitability of 'possessive individualism' (the belief that society is no more than a series of relations between proprietors, and the state solely a contractual device for the defence of property-owners). Although there are ideological divisions between revolutionary and revisionist socialism, socialists share the view that for society to progress there must be some alteration in property relations to achieve a more rational and equitable distribution of resources.

Although political economists such as Francis Fukuyama were mistaken to predict the 'end of history' in the early 1990s, there can be little doubt that collectivist solutions to the problems of modern industrial society have lost much of their former appeal among intellectuals and ordinary voters. In some European countries this has led to increasing support for radical–populist parties that advocate a post-socialist alternative to neoliberal capitalism.

Key issues and debates
- the socialist theory of equality;
- the meaning of collectivism and its implications for the state;
- the socialist theory of needs and welfare;
- utopian socialism;
- Marxism and the communist experiment;
- revisionism and social democracy; and
- neorevisionism.

2 Core ideas of socialism

2.1 The plasticity of human nature

Socialists agree with liberals that human nature can be improved but reject the liberal view of humans as self-interested egoists. Socialists believe that human nature is plastic or malleable: although there is an inherent continuity in the way humans think and act, human nature is susceptible to modification. What we call human nature is not a fixed quantity but a *historical* category, which reflects changes in the economic and cultural development of capitalism.

From this perspective, socialists maintain that individuals are 'corrupted' by the historical conditions into which they are born, which they would not have chosen if they had had an opportunity to decide for themselves. This argument was famously advanced by **utopian socialists** such as Jean-Jacques Rousseau (1712–78), who argued that bourgeois civilisation had undermined the 'nobility' of mankind, and who believed in a hypothetical state of nature as a normative guide. Yet this is a problematic view: it assumes that

humans could retrace their steps and reconstruct a pre-political state of nature based on an ethic of human self-love and empathy rather than pride and competitiveness.

Revolutionary socialists dismiss utopian socialism as wishful thinking, and focus instead on the links between capitalist exchange and human moral psychology. They suggest that there is a direct link between the socio-economic structure of society and human personality. This view was developed by Karl Marx (1818–83), who argued that the relations into which men enter in the organisation of economic life determine the values, ideas and character of individuals in societies.

2.2 Collectivism

Socialism is based on a belief in the superiority of the community or group over the individual, and socialists emphasise collectivist solutions to the problems of social and economic organisation. In this respect, socialists advance a *rationalist* belief in the possibility of cooperation as an alternative to the wastefulness of competitive exchange and private production for the sake of private profit.

All socialists subscribe to the idea of group membership, according to which humans are primarily social beings: mankind is a social animal, and can only achieve greatness and evolve through community, cooperation and division of labour. This perspective privileges collective endeavour over bourgeois individualism, the emphasis being on positive freedom rather than negative freedom.

However, some radical socialists — particularly Marxist–Leninists — argue that cooperation cannot be achieved in the absence of political leadership (the '**vanguard** party'). For this reason, Marxist–Leninists believe in state planning to coordinate collective activity and accelerate economic and social development, to 'overtake capitalism without catching up'.

For critics of socialism such as Hayek, the implications of **collectivism** for the state are extremely dangerous. On the one hand, collectivism negates the principle of possessive individualism (according to which individuals should have exclusive rights over the use of their own property); on the other hand, collectivism is impossible to implement without violence, leading to the expansion of the state as a totalitarian structure controlling the political and economic life of society. The most obvious examples of this are Stalinism and Maoism.

2.3 Equality

Socialists are primarily concerned with the issue of *equality*, which is understood in socio-economic terms as *equality of outcomes*. Whereas liberals advocate a formal definition of equality, e.g. equality before the law/equality of opportunity, socialists maintain that equality is meaningless unless it involves equal access to resources and other primary goods, regardless of individual ability or social privilege.

The socialist critique of liberal theories of equality works on the assumption that formal equality promotes equal opportunities, but ignores the *underlying inequalities in society based on unequal access to resources*. Such unequal access to resources is caused by 'inherited privilege', i.e. by the fact that many individuals who possess economic power do so only because they acquired it in the form of inherited capital. By calling for an equality of outcomes, socialists reject the libertarian conservative acceptance of natural inequality between individuals as a convenient distortion of the truth.

Socialists recognise that many individuals are self-made through their own labour, but criticise the fact that possession of private property leads to undeserved inherited advantages among upper-income groups because those with property inevitably pass on accumulated wealth to their children, and thus reproduce the existing class structure.

An example used by socialists to justify this view is the impact of education on the life-chances of individuals. Socialists concede that some children are naturally more intelligent than others (and are therefore more likely to succeed under whatever circumstances). Yet they insist that unequal access to education is still a cause of structural inequalities. This is particularly the case in capitalist societies where those from privileged backgrounds are able to take advantage of the benefits of private education, while the majority must make do with inferior state education.

2.4 Needs

All forms of socialism promote human welfare. Socialists argue that poverty is the greatest social evil, and that all societies must be judged by how they treat their weakest members. However, there is an important distinction between socialists and communists in relation to equality. Parliamentary socialists have traditionally strived to increase the economic welfare of the working class. In alliance with moderate liberals, they have fought to alleviate urban poverty and deprivation by addressing the needs of workers through the introduction of social welfare, state pensions schemes and a limited redistribution of wealth.

In the Soviet Union, China and Eastern Europe, communists replaced the free market with state planning. Although the communist economic system was by Western standards highly inefficient and environmentally damaging, it did achieve a form of *material* equality through state provision of goods and services, and through a policy of 'levelling from below'.

2.5 Common ownership

Socialists criticise the injustice of private property, arguing that wealth is produced by the community as a whole rather than individuals acting alone. The socialist critique of private property is based not on simple resentment or envy, but on a belief that *private ownership creates the conditions for human inequality*. This view was developed into a systematic critique of capitalism by Marx, who believed that private ownership of the means of production leads to the disempowerment of workers.

However, there is no single perspective on private property within the broad family of ideologies that make up socialism. Although most socialists agree that private owner-ship makes equality impossible, different thinkers have approached the problem in different ways:

- Utopian socialists such as Pierre-Joseph Proudhon (1809–65) criticised private property for moralistic reasons. According to Proudhon, 'all property is theft', and no logical or ethical justification can be made for the view that if 'all men were equal, nobody would work'. There is no 'natural right' to property, he argued, because claims to ownership are really little more than the 'creation of something out of nothing'. The only true value is human industry, which allows humans through their labour to transform nature into objects of utility.

- A very different perspective is offered by Marx, who highlighted the *structuring* role of private property in class societies. In *Capital*, Marx argued that private property has a central significance: all wealth is derived from labour, and ownership of the means of production gives capitalists the ability to exploit labour under intensive conditions. For Marx, capital is formed through the accumulation of surplus value, which the capitalist retains after paying the worker a wage. Workers produce a surplus of value for their employer above what they require to live, and this 'alienated' labour is the real source of capital. Hence emancipation is contingent not just on the overthrow of the 'ruling class', but on the abolition of private ownership as the source of alienated labour.
- For revisionist social democrats, the structuring function of private property is less relevant. Social democrats do not see the need to abolish private ownership, but aim to make capitalism fairer through such methods as progressive taxation. They advocate a qualified acceptance of capitalism, rather than its abolition. The point is to humanise capitalism through limited redistribution and other means designed to compensate for the undeserved social disadvantages caused by differential property ownership.

In the UK in the 1950s, experiments in public ownership led to the creation of monopolies such as British Rail and British Steel, which were managed in the national interest. In Eastern Europe, by contrast, the communist experiment in state planning had mixed results. On the one hand, communists created a more egalitarian society in which wealth was administered in the interests of the majority; on the other hand, industry was less efficient and economic and political power was concentrated in the hands of a new elite of state administrators.

3 *Utopian socialism*

For socialists in the early nineteenth century, liberalism was seen critically as the 'ideology of the factory owner', legitimising the exploitation of workers who were forced to sell their labour and work in dehumanising conditions for the benefit of capitalists. Early socialists had a romantic outlook, and reacted against the industrialisation of Europe and the social misery this caused.

Thinkers such as Charles Fourier (1772–1837), Robert Owen (1771–1858) and Proudhon adopted what Marx termed a 'utopian' perspective. That is, they tried to imagine an ideal world where cooperative communities could live without the harmful effects of industrial capitalism by relying on uncoerced solidarity. This world-view owes much to the ideas of Rousseau.

Rousseau argued that 'Man is born free and everywhere is in chains'. This has been interpreted to mean that, although mankind is born with great potential, humans are constrained by the inequality and hypocrisy of the society into which they are born, but which they did not actively choose and would not have chosen if they had been given a choice. How people live is determined by an accident of birth, which gives some people wealth at the expense of others.

Utopian socialists such as Robert Owen believed that the negative effects of capitalism could be addressed by reducing the size of industrial empires, and by encouraging people to live in small, self-regulating communities in which human communication is still possible. Owen understood the potential of industrialisation for improving human life, but also saw the dangers it posed for society by breaking down communities,

traditions and social structures through rapid urbanisation. He set up an experimental community in the United States (New Lanarkshire) in which **cooperation** replaced competition as the ordering principle of social organisation.

The main problem with utopian socialism is that it ignores mankind's tendency to go beyond the limits of what is given in order to expand available wealth and knowledge — even where this results in disharmony and conflict. Utopian socialists tend to create 'static' models of ideal societies, based on abstract ideals rather than scientific premises, which amount to little more than speculation.

The harshest critics of utopian socialism are not liberals or conservatives but Marxists, who point to the futility of utopian speculation and wishful thinking. Marx himself was scathing about the anarchistic tendencies and implications of Proudhon's philosophy, which, although directed against private property, amounted to little more than a call for the destruction of the state in all its forms. This is seen as irrational by Marxists who invest revolutionary potential in the idea of a qualitatively different 'workers' state'.

Note Like Engels, Owen was a factory owner who saw for himself the horrors of industrial capitalism. Unlike Engels, however, he advocated philanthropic reformism rather than revolution.

4 Marxism

4.1 Philosophical origins

The philosophical basis of Marxism lies in a materialist theory of history, which Marx developed in opposition to Georg Hegel (1770–1831). However, Marx was also an economist and political thinker who criticised the English political economists and French utopian socialists. In *A Contribution to the Critique of Political Economy*, Marx stated:

'My inquiry led me to the conclusion that neither the legal relations nor political forms could be comprehended whether by themselves or on the basis of a so-called general development of the human mind, but that on the contrary, they originate in the material conditions of life, the totality of which Hegel, following the English and French thinkers of the eighteenth century, embraced with the term 'civil society'; that the anatomy of this civil society has to be sought in political economy.'

Marx was indebted not only to socialist thinkers but to the leading bourgeois political economists of his day. Classical Marxism can be understood as a synthesis of three intellectual traditions, which Marx fused into a general critique of capitalist society.

German idealism

Marx's theory of history derives from a critical reading of Hegel, who developed a form of 'dialectical' reasoning based on the assumption that progress is dependent on the continual emergence, growth and overcoming of contradictions. Hegel argued that history is nothing more than the continual unfolding of 'spirit' (*Geist*). According to this view, the essence of 'spirit' is freedom, and world history can be seen as a stage-by-stage unfolding of spirit within successive civilisations. Hegel understood change as a process of negation, where each stage of historical development involves the negation of a previous stage, which outlives its original purpose and contains the seeds of its own destruction.

French socialism

Marx was impressed by the rationalistic ideas of Rousseau and Claude Henri de Saint-Simon (1760–1825). He agreed with Rousseau that the origins of inequality in society lie in the acquisition and accumulation of private property by a few individuals, but rejected moralistic arguments against capitalism, arguing that it is futile to construct abstract Utopias based on the assumption of human sentiment or **altruism**. Instead he developed a 'scientific' theory of history, according to which socialism can only come into existence at the appropriate historical time. Marx understood capitalism as a *necessary stage of development* through which all societies must pass in order to create the conditions for the inevitable transition to socialism. This is because capitalism vastly increases the productive capacity of society, and only when society has reached a higher level of economic and cultural development is it possible to organise the economic life of society on a collectivist basis.

English political economy

Marx was also influenced by the work of the English and Scottish political economists, notably Adam Smith and David Ricardo (1772–1823). In classical political economy, capitalism functions by continually increasing productivity through a system of competitive exchange. Capital is created through a more efficient exploitation of resources and through comparative advantage, while economic growth is based on the expansion of new markets for commodities. Marx criticised these economists for understating the role of *labour* in the accumulation of capital, and argued that the source of all wealth in society is the labour-power of workers, which is transformed into surplus value through labour intensification and division of labour.

4.2 Economic determinism

Marx substituted a materialist theory of progress for Hegel's idealist approach. Whereas Hegel saw history in terms of the movement of world-spirit, Marx located historical progress in the material sphere, arguing that all progress is ultimately a function of economic development. 'In the social production of their existence,' he argued, 'men inevitably enter into definite relations, which are independent of their will... The totality of these relations of production constitutes the economic structure of society, the real foundation, on which arises a legal and political superstructure, and to which correspond definite forms of social consciousness.'

Marx's **economic determinism** amounts to a straightforward claim, namely that the economic base of society (*the productive forces*) determines the political and ideological superstructure (*the relations of production*). It is not consciousness that determines being but being that determines consciousness: our political beliefs and values are generated in response to our changing economic and material needs. This theory of society can be represented in the following topographical form:

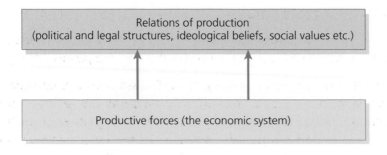

Figure 1

Marx saw human history as determined by modes of production, and divided history into stages, e.g. tribal society, slave-owning society, feudalism and capitalism, each of which is based on a specific mode of production. The transition from one stage of history to another is brought about by increasing contradictions between the productive forces and the relations of production, where the laws and ideas that govern society (the political–ideological 'superstructure') no longer correspond with the development of the productive forces (the 'economic base').

The point of Marx's argument is that, as society's productive forces develop, they clash with the existing relations of production, which serve to constrain their growth. Capitalism becomes like a straitjacket, constraining rather than facilitating progress.

From this perspective, the rate of economic development in society outstrips the rate of political and ideological development *because the political system serves to preserve the interests of the ruling class*. This lack of correspondence fuels crisis tendencies, and the purpose of activism is to hasten the transition to socialism by promoting class consciousness through mass mobilisation and education — a view rejected by Lenin, who emphasised revolution.

Note Orthodox Marxists such as Karl Kautsky (1854–1938) assumed that the evolution of society towards socialism was inevitable. But communists such as Lenin adopted a more voluntarist approach, stressing the importance of revolutionary activism. Lenin believed that capitalism was nowhere more secure than in the context of a democratic republic, and for this reason denounced Kautsky as a 'renegade'.

4.3 Class struggle

In *The Communist Manifesto*, Marx and Engels assert that 'The history of all hitherto existing society is the history of **class struggles**'. Marx initially saw the bourgeoisie as a revolutionary class, but concluded that it had become a barrier to progress. The interests of the bourgeoisie (private ownership for private profit) contradict the collective interests of society, leading to economic crisis and political unrest.

Marx identified the proletariat as the new revolutionary force that would overthrow capitalism and create the conditions for a new society based on social ownership. He predicted that the conflict between the bourgeoisie and the proletariat would intensify and lead to revolution in which workers would overcome '**false consciousness**', the capitalist state, and create a 'commonwealth of free producers'. In effect, capitalism contains the 'seeds of its own destruction' by creating a new class of propertyless workers whose interests are antagonistic to capital.

4.4 Criticisms of Marx's theory

Marx's theory is too deterministic. Although Marx insists that mankind makes its *own* history, he places too much stress on the economic causes of social and political change.

Marx underestimates the long-term viability of capitalism. Marx underestimates the capacity of capitalism to overcome contradictions such as the falling rate of profit and overproduction. On the one hand, capitalism is reinvigorated by technological innovations that reduce the need for skilled labour. On the other hand, consumerism 'creates' new needs, ensuring new markets for its commodities.

Marx was wrong to predict the polarisation of society into two irreconcilable classes. The advanced industrialised nations of the West are *stratified* rather than *polarised*. Furthermore, the middle classes own property, and there is a high level of social mobility as a result of education and other mechanisms of distribution.

'False consciousness' alone fails to explain why workers adapt to the capitalist system. Although the concept of false consciousness appears to explain why workers do not rebel, it has been criticised for underestimating the extent to which workers identify positively with the capitalist system. Capitalism breaks down ties of solidarity between workers by promoting self-interest, which encourages complacency about the viability of collective action.

The working class in the rich countries has benefited from capitalism. Marx overestimated the extent to which workers would be impoverished by exploitation. This is because he underestimated the extent to which reformist socialists would adapt to the rational requirements of the capitalist system. It is also in the interests of the state and employers that workers benefit from prosperity and have access to welfare and legal protection.

4.5 Marxist theories of the state

In his sociological writings Marx argued that the political organisation of society (the state) is structurally and ideologically determined by economic interests. Politics does not take place in a social vacuum, but reflects the relative power of socio-economic groups which support rival factions in the state to advance their own agendas. Marxist theories of the state can be divided into two main types:

- *Instrumental theories.* In Marx's early works, the state is viewed as the *instrument* of class rule. Marx argued that the political and ideological superstructure of society reflects the interests of the *economically dominant class*. Hence in capitalist societies the state is controlled by representatives of the bourgeoisie, and acts on behalf of its economic interests. According to this view, the state lacks any autonomous role in society.
- *Structuralist theories.* In his later works, Marx developed a more sociological approach to the state. He concluded that the political organisation of society can develop a life of its own (in the sense that it does more than merely pass legislation to suit capitalists). However, the state remains in essence an expression of the *balance of class forces in society*. This view was developed by Nicos Poulantzas (1936–79), who argued that the state assumes a semi-autonomous role in society. Poulantzas concluded that the main function of the state is to secure the necessary political conditions for the reproduction of the capitalist system.

Marx assumed that the capitalist state would eventually be replaced by a dictatorship of the proletariat — a temporary state that would come into being during the transition from capitalism to communism. This would, theoretically, be a democratic dictatorship because it would be supported by the most progressive elements of the people, and would act against the people's true enemies. Once class enemies had been defeated, the state would no longer serve any purpose and would wither away (but history has shown this assumption to be an illusion).

4.6 Differences between classical Marxism and Leninism

Although Marx believed that the dictatorship of the proletariat would be temporary, he was vague about the reality of a post-capitalist state, and critics have argued that this

has legitimised the abuses of power carried out by revolutionary socialists. It is only in the work of V. I. Lenin (1870–1924) that the idea of revolutionary dictatorship was fully examined.

Leninism differs from classical Marxism in three main respects:

- Lenin developed the idea of the 'vanguard party'. With a view to Russian conditions, he argued that the vanguard (an elite caste of professional revolutionaries) could compensate for the weaknesses of the workers' movement by assuming a leadership role. In his view, social democrats such as Kautsky had abandoned the revolutionary aim of Marxism in favour of a gradualist approach based on a political compromise between the progressive bourgeoisie and the labour movement.
- Lenin believed that, rather than abolish the state, the vanguard should adapt the 'best parts' of the capitalist state to suit the purposes of the new revolutionary order. The main purpose of this was to ensure the survival of an administrative apparatus, which the Bolsheviks saw as essential for the construction of a post-revolutionary order. For this reason, anarchists have been deeply critical of Leninism, which, they contend, leads to a dictatorship over the proletariat.
- Whereas Marx believed in overcoming the capitalist division of labour, allowing workers to take control of the means of production, Lenin argued that the dictatorship of the proletariat should reintroduce traditional forms of industrial organisation and management in order to increase the productivity of labour.

4.7 Stalinism

Marxism gave rise to a number of revolutionary socialist movements in the twentieth century, including Leninism, Stalinism and Maoism. The most successful of these was Stalinism in the USSR. Although the Chinese Communist Party is still in power, it abandoned Maoism in the late 1970s after the failure of the Cultural Revolution.

Some observers see Stalinism as a form of 'totalitarianism', which implies a totalising form of ideology used to legitimise a system of absolute power. However, Stalinism can more accurately be seen as an alternative model of industrial development. Despite the immense human suffering caused by terror and forced labour, Russia was transformed in three decades from an agrarian society into an industrial superpower.

In economic terms, Stalinism represents an extreme type of bureaucratic collectivism in which the class of capitalist owners is replaced by a party-state elite as the 'administrators of historical necessity'. The Communist Party maintained complete control over the economy, which was based on 'production for the sake of the plan', and which was riddled with inefficiency and corruption. Under Stalin and his successors, Marxism–Leninism was transformed into a legitimation device — an ideological model emulated by the satellite states of Eastern Europe after 1945.

The Soviet Union provided a model for the Chinese Revolution under Mao Zedong (1893–1976), and for anti-colonial movements in Vietnam, Algeria, Cuba, Cambodia, Yemen, Angola and Mozambique, which saw communism as an alternative to integration into the international capitalist system (see Chapter 5).

Leon Trotsky (1879–1940) argued that Stalinism was a distortion of Leninism, but many historians disagree. They stress that Stalinism could not have happened without Lenin's singular revolutionary vision and ruthless leadership style. Apologists for Lenin often forget the number of innocent people who died during the Red Terror while Lenin was still leader, as well as his determination to 'export' the revolution (and therefore Soviet influence) by force.

The collapse of communism can be explained by the paralysis of the Soviet economy. Despite many significant achievements, state socialism promised more than it could deliver, and the difference between living standards in Eastern and Western Europe became a source of political embarrassment. This was nowhere more apparent in Poland, where in 1980 workers brought the entire country to a halt with the Solidarity protests.

The crisis of the Soviet system was graphically illustrated by the Chernobyl disaster of 1985, as well as the failure of collectivised agriculture to satisfy the material needs of the Soviet people. Under Khrushchev and Brezhnev, the Communist Party tried to legitimise its power using the slogan 'developed socialism', but the only real justification for the perpetuation of the system was the survival of the ruling oligarchy itself.

Note The Stalinist model was applied in Eastern Europe after 1945 with mixed results. Some critics suggest it was a logical response to the need for reconstruction and development in the region, but this ignores the social and political consequences of four decades of political repression and economic incompetence.

5 Parliamentary socialism

In contrast to revolutionary socialists, parliamentary socialists advocate a *revisionist* strategy by embracing the politics of **gradualism** and reform. Their aim is to create socialism democratically, by achieving a parliamentary majority and using the state as an instrument of collective organisation. The origins of parliamentary socialism lie in the revisionist critique of Marxism by theorists such as Eduard Bernstein (1850–1932), who rejected Marx's view that capitalism would inevitably collapse under the weight of its own contradictions.

Bernstein argued that socialist parties should ally themselves with progressive bourgeois parties to form a liberal/socialist parliamentary bloc, which the socialists would inevitably come to dominate as a result of electoral superiority. In this way, it was argued, socialism could be achieved by democratic rather than violent means.

Revisionism led to the rise of moderate centre-left parties such as the Labour Party in Britain and the Social Democrats (SPD) in Germany. As moderates, these movements accepted the existence of the capitalist system, but sought to curb the negative effects of free trade through state intervention, limited redistribution and social welfare. This led to a new 'politics of gradualism', i.e. a situation where socialists work within the existing system to achieve more limited goals.

5.1 Democratic socialism

This term is used to explain the ideology of socialist parties and movements that are opposed to capitalism and seek to create socialism by democratic (evolutionary) rather than violent (revolutionary) means. A good example of this type of movement is the Fabians in Britain in the inter-war years, a group of left-wing intellectuals and political leaders who rejected Marxism, which they viewed as excessively deterministic. The Fabians believed that a progressive alternative to capitalism required both economic modernisation and cultural development, which presupposed a shift away from competitive resource allocation towards collective cooperation and organisation.

They also believed that the state could exert greater control over investment, without abolishing all private property and private exchange, by placing the 'commanding heights of the economy' (key industries) in public hands.

The main goals of democratic socialism include:
- social equality;
- mixed economy leading to nationalisation;
- state regulation of the free market;
- universal welfare;
- state education;
- municipal subsidised housing; and
- cultural advancement of the working class.

5.2 Social democracy

The difference between democratic socialism and social democracy may seem obscure, but is fundamental for understanding the fate of socialism in Western Europe in the twentieth century. Whereas *democratic socialists* promote a gradual transition to socialism, *social democrats* typically opt for a qualified acceptance of capitalism. This has led critics of parliamentary socialism such as Miliband to argue that social democrats seek only to reform the political system while leaving the class structure and political economy of capitalism unchanged.

From a Marxist perspective, the failure to achieve socialism by democratic means stems from the nature of capitalist societies, which Gramsci explained using Marx's dominant ideology thesis. According to Gramsci, capitalism becomes entrenched in the value-system of modern society: the system acquires legitimacy because it is literally 'taken for granted' — as if it were the natural order of things rather than a stage of human development. This leads either to fatalistic acceptance of the system or to false consciousness. Simply winning elections is insufficient because the state is dominated by non-socialist elites that co-opt reformists into their ruling strategy, thereby obstructing change.

Marxists argue that this paradox is exemplified by the constraints imposed on the Labour Party in Britain in the 1970s by right-wing elements in the British state and economy, which sought to prevent Labour from implementing radical policies such as the abolition of private education. They also argue that parliamentary socialists succumb to the very political culture they once opposed. By standing for elected office, they become practitioners of the 'politics of compromise', which divorces parliamentary leaders from their true constituency.

An alternative explanation for the decline of social democracy lies in the nature of inter-party competition and the tendency of parties to adjust their policies in order to win voters in the political marketplace. In the immediate post-war era, the Labour Party was still identified with one section of society, the industrial working class. It has since been forced to broaden its appeal by adopting pragmatic policies acceptable to middle-class and elite interests. This has occurred because the traditional constituency of the left has shrunk. Until the 1960s, manual workers represented 45% of the electorate, a figure that has rapidly diminished with the rise of the new middle classes and the decline of manufacturing industries. Growing affluence has led to increased integration of workers within the 'rising expectations logic' of capitalism. This has resulted in changes in voters' preferences, and a breakdown of old class loyalties.

Key terms and concepts

Altruism	Regard for others as a principle of action
Class struggle	The historic conflict between oppressors and oppressed that has continued from ancient times until the present day; under capitalism, class struggle reaches its highest stage
Collectivism	Political principle that gives the collective group priority over the individual
Cooperation	The idea that social and political goals can be achieved more effectively if individuals agree to work together and share resources rather than compete
Economic determinism	The view that social, political and ideological phenomena are determined in the final analysis by changes in the means of production
False consciousness	Marxist concept which holds that workers are falsely encouraged to identify with the values of capitalism, even though the logic of the system is contrary to their real interests
Fraternity	The socialist ideal of 'brotherhood' — a body of people united in its interests and goals
Gradualism	A cautious form of democratic socialism committed to gradual social reform and alliance with progressive liberal parties
Historical materialism	Marxist philosophy which holds that social, political and intellectual development is determined in the final instance by changes in the forces and relations of production
Positive equality	Material equality (equality of outcomes rather than equality defined in a formal sense)
Revisionism	Historical tradition within parliamentary socialism, characterised by the tendency of socialist parties to abandon radical political goals for the sake of limited reform
Social exclusion	The exclusion of individuals and communities living below the poverty line from effective participation in the political, economic and cultural life of society
Social justice	The belief that politics should be concerned with removing the undeserved constraints that prevent some members of society from realising their potential
Utopian socialism	Socialism established by capitalists' peaceful surrender of the means of production in response to moral persuasion
Vanguard	Leninist principle of political organisation, based on the leadership of a professional revolutionary elite (commissars)

CHAPTER 4 Anarchism

1 Introduction

Anarchism is based on the belief that all human association should be voluntary rather than coercive. Anarchists believe there is an essential contradiction between authority and **autonomy** because, once individuals become dependent on the normative guidance of power-holders, they relinquish their capacity for moral self-direction. Anarchists also believe that, despite the claims of liberals and conservatives, all forms of organised political authority are founded on violence, but this 'originary violence' is cloaked in constitutional legality to disguise its true nature.

The word anarchy means literally 'no government', but, contrary to popular stereotypes, anarchists should not simply be summed up as destructive nihilists. The myth of the bomb-throwing fanatic in Joseph Conrad's *The Secret Agent* is a relic of the nineteenth century, reflecting Victorian anxieties of social disorder and revolution.

In the most basic sense, anarchists seek to replace the coercive authority of the state and other traditional institutions with alternative forms of social organisation based on voluntary participation and democratic decision-making. Although communist anarchists share certain Marxist assumptions about capitalism, they reject the socialist belief in the state as a means for organising the collective life of society. From an anarchist perspective, it is the existence of the state itself that is the primary issue.

Note Above all, anarchists reject the legitimacy of the state as a structure of domination.

Key issues and debates
- the link between anarchism and utopianism;
- the contradiction between authority and autonomy;
- the anarchist critique of the state;
- the differences between individualist and collectivist anarchism;
- the distinction between anarchism and libertarianism;
- the distinction between anarchism and Marxism; and
- the viability of a future stateless society.

2 Core ideas of anarchism

2.1 Moral autonomy

Crispin Sartwell, author of *Against the State*, argues that anarchism 'serves the same function in political theory that scepticism serves in the theory of knowledge'. Whereas the sceptic rejects foundational principles of knowledge — principles designed to establish the certainty of our beliefs — the anarchist rejects traditional assumptions concerning what human nature is and what human beings are capable of achieving.

Most obviously, anarchists reject the Hobbesian argument that all rational individuals would voluntarily enter into a binding contract with a sovereign in order to achieve lasting collective peace and security. In Hobbes's moral theory, humans are portrayed as vulnerable to an 'excess of appetite', and no person living in a state of nature can be sure that their neighbours will not — if given the opportunity — murder them or rob them of their possessions.

Anarchists deny Hobbes's assertion, not because humans are saintly creatures but because they are corrupted by the world into which they are born, one which, if given the choice, they would not have chosen for themselves. It is perfectly rational for individuals to be ruthless exploiters or violent oppressors if such conduct is rewarded by the society or culture in question.

Perhaps the most famous anarchist philosopher of human nature is the English writer William Godwin (1756–1836), who understood human nature as 'malleable'. In common with many rationalists of his day, Godwin believed that human nature is not fixed but culturally formed by the influences to which all humans are exposed. These differ from one epoch to another, hence it is nonsense to categorise human nature as a constant, non-varying phenomenon. Godwin's optimistic view that human nature is not only malleable but perfectible is justified in two ways:

- all humans possess a capacity for reason; and
- reason implies the possibility of universal benevolence.

Although humans are 'corrupted' by the environment in which they find themselves (it is rational to adapt to externally imposed expectations even if we do not agree with them), each generation has a chance to improve upon previous generations and to increase the sum of human welfare through right action. The process of enlightenment may take generations, but human beings should eventually reach a stage where the power of reason is sufficient to outweigh prejudice, superstition and tradition.

This rose-tinted Enlightenment view of human nature and historical progress is not shared by all anarchists, however:

- Proudhon did not believe in perfectibility. On the contrary, he accepted that humans are capable of evil and inclined towards self-preservation. Like Marx, however, he also believed that the chief cause of moral corruptibility is the institution of private property, which distorts human relations.
- Murray Rothbard emphasised the **egoism** and legitimate private interest of human beings. From an anarcho–capitalist perspective, moralistic attacks on private property are pointless because all humans seek security and personal advancement. Rothbard denied that a revolution in human nature would be possible through moral perfectibility, but instead a more limited goal, namely that anarchism could maximise opportunities for the good and minimise opportunities for the bad.

2.2 Natural order

A natural order is characterised by *peaceful cooperation*. Anarchists maintain that humans have the ability to create non-authoritarian forms of social organisation based on natural order, as an alternative to the prevailing institutional form of the state. They insist that beyond the positive law of individual states there are overarching moral or natural laws, and that truly free individuals are those who would logically favour reason, compassion and **solidarity** not because they are told to do so, but because — having become enlightened — they would have no reason not to.

However, natural order implies a further assumption, namely that humans can achieve an equitable distribution of resources in order to avoid the Hobbesian 'war of all against all'. The question anarchists seek to resolve is how to ensure that an anarchist society would be both peaceful and orderly:

Anarchism presupposes a society without submission to coercive authority, where voluntary agreements are made and entered into between consenting individuals to resolve coordination problems. The result of the growing number of agreements between individuals is enhanced civilisation, which for most of human history has evolved in the absence of an organised state.

In anarchist theory, the credibility of individuals with decision-making power should be based on the respect-worthiness of their actions, rather than on habitual deference or obedience towards authority. Respect for decisions taken in the interests of social coordination must be voluntarily given by those who wish to participate, and all those who remain unreconciled should have the option to leave.

At the same time, those individuals who aspire to leadership positions should do so for purely functional reasons, e.g. because they are efficient managers, rather than to dominate others. To ensure that power-holders do not become accustomed to giving orders, regular rotation of command positions must take place and regular democratic affirmation of executive decisions must be routine.

Natural order presupposes that order must be more *spontaneous* if general agreement is to be reached peacefully between a collective and the individuals within that collective. Organising people into a community where peace can prevail means establishing bonds of trust and/or solidarity between cooperating individuals before expanding these relations to include a wider community of participants. Order based on an expanding network of peaceful exchange is thus derived from the ground up rather than on the basis of hierarchy.

2.3 Opposition to authority

Liberals defend 'legitimate authority' by arguing that it renders coercion unnecessary where citizens recognise an unconditional obligation to obey the law. In liberal political theory, there is a philosophical distinction between power and authority: power is the capacity to rule, while authority is the right to rule.

As Professor David Beetham argues, legitimate political authority is not legitimate simply because people believe it to be so, but because it provides a normative basis for the exercise of power. In the absence of legitimate authority, rulers inevitably resort to more violent forms of propaganda and control to maintain stability.

This argument is rejected by anarchists because, they argue, the veil of authority conceals the *actual* force necessary to establish political order. In anarchist theory, the evolution of modern society is founded on what Michel Foucault (1926–84) termed a 'succession of violences', i.e. the emergence of apparatuses of domination, which control and govern the life of individuals in the most profound and intimate ways.

Anarchists reject liberal justifications of authority because these are seen to contradict the capacity of the individual to achieve moral autonomy. They also reject conservative theories of authority as normative guidance, because norms and values are not value-neutral. Rather, they reflect the ideological prejudices of ruling elites whose interests are legitimised through the apparently neutral institutions of law, custom and convention.

Recognition of shared norms may be essential for organising mutually beneficial forms of social coordination, e.g. to reduce risk and error; but, according to anarchists, the enforcement of law, custom and convention in the absence of actual agreement reflects the *social power* rather than *authority* of traditional elites.

2.4 Anti-statism

It follows from this that anarchists reject normative justifications of the state as a necessary and inevitable feature of human social and political organisation. The state is seen as a source of oppression rather than empowerment, and anarchists oppose institutions of organised government such as the police, the law, the courts, the military and state education. These agencies are used to dominate individuals, and the increasing dependence of citizens on the state prevents them from creating appropriate conditions under which they might be capable of governing themselves.

Anarchism is thus directed against the negative consequences of the state as a form of tyranny which has no absolute or even conditional right to exist. As David Miller, author of *Anarchism*, argues, there are four features of the state to which anarchists object:

- That the state is sovereign, and claims the authority to determine the social, legal and political affairs of citizens without their explicit consent. Although elections may be held to legitimise rulers, citizens cannot be allowed to challenge the supremacy of the state itself.
- That the state is compulsory: that all citizens have an unconditional obligation to accept its existence and increasing presence in organised social life. However, anarchists argue that contract theory provides an inadequate justification for political obligation, while fairness and reciprocity arguments fail to establish an unconditional moral duty to obey the law.
- That the state is monopolistic. As Max Weber (1864–1920) argued, all states claim a monopoly of force within their borders, making it illegal for alternative forms of social organisation to compete with the state for control over territory and resources.
- That the state is a distinct body in that it stands above society in a relationship of domination. The state employs a large number of people who act as its agents, monitoring, surveying, recording and regulating the natural social roles and functions of human agents.

The authority of the modern state is based on legislation passed by successive governments, who determine the content and nature of laws within the jurisdiction of the state concerned. This law is known as 'positive law', because it is 'posited' or created by legal authorities, not because it is based on considerations of morality or natural justice. For anarchists, this is a consequence of the artificial division of humanity into states: the state effectively replaces humanity and overrides all natural laws and human customs. As such, the state usurps or overrides the (potential) moral autonomy of individuals. By handing over their sovereignty to the state, individuals lose the will and ability to make decisions for themselves and to take responsibility for their own welfare. Although citizens retain a measure of personal liberty in liberal-democratic societies, they are subject to increasing forms of surveillance and control by state institutions.

The philosophical anarchist tradition

It is often assumed that anarchists conceive of freedom in a purely negative sense, i.e. as a variety of extreme libertarianism. If this were all anarchism entailed, it could simply be described as an extreme offshoot of libertarianism. However, the anarchist concept of freedom also entails a positive dimension. Anarchists wish to promote the freedom to act — not in accordance with an everyday, empirical self, i.e. a self defined in objective terms, but with the 'authentic self'.

This authentic self is defined as that part of an individual's personality that characterises him or her most fundamentally. Authenticity depends on possession of two things:

- *critical rationality* (the capacity of individuals to judge or act only for those reasons that are their own); and
- *virtue* (the capacity of individuals to will morally right action).

The ultimate goal of philosophical anarchism is to counter traditional arguments in favour of political obligation, and to establish the appropriate conditions under which individuals might achieve autonomy as self-legislating moral agents. Before we can do this, we have to recognise the fundamental contradiction that exists between authority and autonomy.

3.1 The liberal justification for political authority

Governments possess authority because they claim a right to rule, and succeed in establishing a legitimate claim to rule. Their citizens acknowledge the governments' power to issue authoritative commands and habitually comply with the requirement to obey the law. According to Joseph Raz, political authority in this sense may not actually be owed a duty of obedience, e.g. if a government acts unconstitutionally; however, there is no such thing as a political authority that does not claim a duty of obedience: all authority claims are based (rightly or wrongly) on this assumption.

Raz defines authority in this sense as the *power to require action*. He argues that effective authority involves content-independent reasons for action, where the opinions or commands of rulers are themselves taken as reason for compliance regardless of the exact grounds upon which the opinions of commands are based. On this view, a reason is content-independent if there is no direct link between the reason given and the action for which it is a reason: we acknowledge people's authority not because of *what* they might command us to do, but simply because they have issued us with a relevant authoritative command. Because they occupy positions of authority, our compliance should be a matter of course.

Justified authority thus works by *excluding private judgement* as a basis for compliance with authoritative commands. Authoritative reasons for compliance do not 'outweigh' competing considerations; rather, they exclude alternative competing considerations as *irrelevant*. This 'surrender of judgement' is justified in two ways:
- in a *minimalist* sense because people usually have no judgement of their own on the merits of performing required actions; or
- in a *maximalist* sense because even if people do have alternative views, these will rarely be sufficient to 'tip the balance' against performing the required act.

This does not mean that those in positions of authority can simply require us to carry out absurd or dangerous acts. All authorities are limited by the kinds of reasons upon which they can rely in making decisions and issuing commands, and by the kinds of reasons their decisions can pre-empt. Raz calls this the 'dependence thesis', namely that all authoritative commands should be based on reasons that already apply independently to subjects, and that are relevant to their action in the circumstances covered by the command. Such commands should encourage subjects to *act in ways in which they might ideally act themselves were they minded to do so.*

3.2 Anarchist objections

Anarchists reject this claim because it eliminates (or at least erodes) the autonomy of agents by overriding or pre-empting private judgement. In anarchist thought, progress is inseparable from the achievement of moral autonomy. If we are to achieve true freedom, we must accept that being responsible for our actions is a consequence of the capacity for choice and a prerequisite for true freedom. According to the anarchist philosopher R. P. Wolff:

> 'Every man who possesses both free will and reason has an obligation to take responsibility for his actions, even though he may not be actively engaged in a continuing process of reflection, investigation, and deliberation about how he ought to act... When we describe someone as a responsible individual, we do not imply that he always does what is right, but only that he does not neglect the duty of attempting to ascertain what is right.'

In this respect, anarchism belongs to the 'perfectionist' tradition of philosophy dating back to Baruch Spinoza (1632–77) and Immanuel Kant (1724–1804). This tradition emphasises the full development of human reason and man's moral nature: *to be fully human is to be fully rational, which is in turn to be virtuous*. The anarchist account of progress is based on a principled faith in the compatibility of scientific and moral values. Anarchists stress that moral autonomy is principally a function of knowledge and therefore open to scientific clarification like anything else.

Wolff concedes the necessity of complying with the law under certain circumstances, and he accepts that in certain cases it is perfectly rational for free individuals to obey the law if the law can be justified in appropriate terms. Nevertheless, he rejects the view that the commands of the state have a *prima facie* binding moral force, i.e. that they should be regarded as grounds for obedience under normal circumstances.

Utilitarian arguments based on the rationality of unconditional obligation to obey the law are also criticised because, although it is true that people are generally more concerned with the pursuit of trivial private advantage than with the welfare of the community, cooperation is still possible in the absence of an authoritative state. As Rolf Sartorius argues, there is no logical correlation between the political authority of the state and the legal obligation of citizens: those in authority positions may correctly claim a moral right to rule, but those under their power cannot, under any philosophically interesting conditions, be said to have a correlative duty to obey the law — which is divorced from the simple virtues of natural justice.

Neither do arguments for political obligation based on fairness, gratitude or reciprocity work because it is impossible to prove whether individuals actively solicited benefits from the state and hence 'owe' a duty to respect authority, or whether they merely passively consumed them because they were available in return for conformity. It is a fact of life in modern states that *opting out of citizenship* is all but impossible. Hence any benefits one receives are really the result of government exercising its monopoly over the use of coercion, most obviously by enforcing compulsory taxation.

For anarchists, there is nothing voluntary or tacit about consent under such conditions because obligation is not based on promise. In fact, the reverse is the case: there is an obligation on the *state* not to usurp or exceed its powers, rather than a *prima facie* political obligation on citizens to obey the law.

3.3 Realist counter-objections

There are problems with this argument, which appears to undermine the possibility of coherent government. For this reason, liberal political theorists object to philosophical anarchism as a **utopian** theory of political organisation.

↳ extreme libertarianism

The common-sense objection

Anarchism appears to be a recipe for extreme subjectivism. If all individuals were to become self-legislating actors — each obeying only those laws that they authentically accepted — coherent government and social order would be impossible. Individuals would have the option of obeying laws they considered just, but ignoring laws they considered unjust, which would undermine the ability of communities to establish rule-based behaviour.

Knowledge does not presuppose moral action

According to this view, anarchists present an overly optimistic assessment of human nature, which contrasts dramatically with the view of more pragmatic thinkers such as Hobbes and Weber. These thinkers stress that there is little to suggest that rationality converges with morality. As Weber argued, science (technical knowledge) can tell us nothing about how we should act (moral values), only how to achieve our ends. History shows that scientific knowledge is not usually employed for ethical purposes.

Perfectionism effectively forces individuals to be free

As the liberal philosopher Isaiah Berlin (1909–97) argued, such elevated concepts of the 'good' can be manipulated and exploited by a dictatorship to force people to act in a certain way, which may actually undermine their liberty. In this sense, he argued, there are similarities between anarchism and other totalitarian ideologies such as Marxism, which begin with high-sounding principles but result in oppression and human misery.

4 *Individualist anarchism*

4.1 Individualist anarchism and libertarianism

Individualist anarchism entails a principled resistance to authority based on negative freedom and an egoistic concern with the self. Like libertarians, individualist anarchists argue that humans should be free to act without constraint or external interference. However, anarchism exceeds libertarianism by calling for a *stateless* society rather than a *minimal* state.

Before examining anarchist arguments in favour of a stateless, individualist society, we must first distinguish between libertarianism and individualist anarchism. In contrast to Murray Rothbard, who believed that a truly libertarian society would be anarchic, Robert Nozick, author of *Anarchy, State, and Utopia*, argued that, even where full respect is given to individuals' negative rights (life, liberty and property), society will inevitably return to some form of 'minarchism' based on a minimal state. Why do libertarians believe this to be the case?

Unlike anarchists, who hold that competing 'protective associations' could replace the state as a provider of economic security and social order, libertarians maintain that a condition of 'minarchy' is preferable because, as Tibor Machan, author of *Libertarianism Defended*, argues:

'When living in communities, dangers from others exist and it is ethically imperative to address these dangers; government, rightly understood, is the institution that specialises in proper protection of individual rights, thus It would be ethical to establish government rather than leaving the task of rights-protection to individuals and agencies lacking the special training to protect rights properly.'

In practical terms, this means that libertarianism remains committed to some variety of universally binding sovereign authority (a minimal state) to ensure adequate protection of negative rights. Although libertarians hold that in a libertarian society no exclusion of competing providers of security can be justified, in reality such a system would be chaotic and more likely to fail than a minarchist system based on a legal authority of last resort.

Ultimately, therefore, libertarian minarchism falls back on the need for some form of central political authority *not* because community life presupposes necessary coercion, but because there will always be a need to use coercion against some individuals who engage in criminal conduct. Despite this, libertarians hold that government need not be oppressive, and need not expand beyond a certain functional role.

This argument is in line with the basic tenets of classical liberalism: a nightwatchman state must not interfere in private transactions, but is an essential organisational system for dealing with rights violations and solving coordination problems. For individualist anarchists, however, this is not enough: the real goal must be to establish non-state-based forms of social and political organisation that prevent the re-emergence of a sovereign entity having control over the body politic.

4.2 Nineteenth-century individualist anarchism

Individualist anarchism takes libertarianism as its starting point, and it is no coincidence that some of the most important thinkers in the libertarian anarchist tradition have emerged from the American libertarian tradition. They see the rights given to individuals in a negative sense, i.e. they are rights that prevent people from doing things to others, rights that allow one to do whatever one wants as long as one does not violate given constraints agreed upon by all members of the community or society. These negative rights include:

- the right not to be killed or assaulted by others;
- the right not to be coerced by the state;
- the right not to have one's property taken; and
- the right to use one's property and oneself in any way that one sees fit so long as one does not violate the rights of another.

These rights are not positive rights, entitling people to certain benefits. Rather, they are rights that protect individuals from others and from unjust interference by the state. Along with a commitment to natural rights, anarcho–individualists also emphasise the importance of personal responsibility, insofar as rational adults are taken to be:

- exclusively responsible for the situation in which they find themselves; and
- responsible for whatever negative outcomes result from their actions.

The primary concerns of individualist anarchism are personal liberty and economic freedom. Implicit in the writings of anarcho–individualists is a belief that the modern state constitutes a threat to the economic sovereignty of private individuals. The state does not simply tax and control the population; rather, it assumes a leadership role over the management of the economy — particularly under conditions of crisis and war.

In the USA, for example, the Federal government began to acquire an interventionist role in the mid-nineteenth century. Following the defeat of the Confederacy, the American political system became more centralised (reducing the legislative autonomy of the states). At the same time, large corporate firms and banks expanded their business activities across the entire nation, creating semi-legal trusts that undermined the economic welfare of small businessmen and farmers.

This encouraged a new form of ideological opposition to statist capitalism based on the central demand for a free economy and a critique of contract theory. Although this ideological current absorbed some ideas from European socialism (from Proudhon rather than Marx), it remained within the *individualist* tradition of resistance to corporate statism. One of the key figures in this movement was Benjamin Tucker (1854–1939), who developed a philosophy of self-government and self-reliance, rejecting bourgeois conformism in favour of autonomy, individual judgement and personal choice.

Note In his writings, Tucker was critical of Marx. He disapproved in particular of the 'state-worship' in German philosophy.

4.3 Equitable exchange

Like Godwin, Tucker held that a new basis of self-regulation and social interdependence could be founded upon the gradual but inevitable expansion of human knowledge. As an economic liberal, Tucker insisted that the only legitimate economic system is one based on private property and exchange, and he opposed egalitarianism as unworkable. He believed that exploitative labour practices should be abolished, but remained committed to the free market as the best means for allocating resources.

Following the example of Josiah Warren (1798–1874), however, Tucker embraced the idea of 'equitable exchange'. According to this idea, the exchange value of commodities should reflect more closely the actual quantity of labour required to produce them. The logic of this was to ensure just remuneration for workers' labour power, and to defend the multitude of small producers and artisans threatened by the development of monopolistic capitalism in the late nineteenth century.

Warren and Tucker both envisaged a more benign form of capitalism based on a free economy — one without state-monopolistic practices. There is more than a degree of romanticism in their work, and their views attracted limited support. Indeed, they appeared anachronistic when viewed against the rapid development of industrial capitalism, which — as Marx predicted — rendered meaningless the speculative idealism of utopian socialists such as Proudhon and Fourier.

4.4 Anarcho–capitalism

Anarcho–individualism in the twentieth century arose largely in response to the development of state-regulated capitalism. In most Western countries, the state has become more and more closely involved in the stabilisation and regulation of the market. The reasons for this are numerous, but the logic of state intervention can be traced back to the problem of 'market failure'. Put simply: there are some goods and services that markets cannot allocate efficiently, but that the state (by means of universal taxation) can.

This problem underlies the collectivist logic of the modern state, which compensates for market failure by providing public goods such as education and health care for all citizens free at the point of delivery (whether they take advantage of these or not). Modern anarcho–individualists criticise the state for invading the individual's private sphere in pursuit of collective solutions to the problems of mass industrial society. Principally, individualist anarchists argue that it is illegitimate for the state to invade people's privacy and impose taxes even where this is carried out for benign paternalist reasons. They contend that 'patterned redistributions' of resources amount to little more than legitimised theft.

Latter-day anarcho–capitalists argue that the very existence of the state testifies to the decreasing freedom of citizens in modern society. From the seventeenth century onwards, the state has gradually come to assume a more invasive and authoritarian role at the expense of individual liberty. Thinkers such as Nozick and Rothbard argue that the state is now engaged in a range of functions that go far beyond what governments were ever meant to do.

In place of the interventionist state, anarcho–capitalists stress the idea of 'proprietism'. In its simplest from, proprietism implies two main components:

- *Establishment of social order on the basis of property rights.* In a hypothetical society based on proprietism, social order would be grounded on the assumption that if all individuals own property then it is in their mutual self-interest to respect the legitimate rights of others to acquire and own property, and to act in accordance with their own rational self-interest. In such a society, rights would be based on legitimate entitlement and 'self-ownership'. Individuals would only pay for goods and services that they voluntarily chose to buy or use, and 'society' as such would cease to be a meaningful concept.
- *Replacement of the state by 'protective associations'.* A further, more radical step would be to replace the existing legal framework of the state with competing protective associations. In traditional political systems, the state maintains its centralised power over society by monopolising the means of coercion and justice. Anarcho–individualists argue that it makes more sense for individuals to organise their own protective associations to defend private property and resolve conflicts. By paying into protective schemes, individuals could obtain security without giving up their individual sovereignty to the state.

These ideas are radical in the extreme, and critics of anarcho–individualism suggest that the existence of multiple protective associations within a single society would be a recipe for legal and administrative chaos for the following reasons:

- Protective associations would be dominated by those who *already* possess wealth and influence. Individuals without property would have little incentive to join such schemes, leaving them insecure and without formal legal protection.
- As libertarians argue, the presence of multiple competing protective associations would necessitate the return of some kind of central authority in order to regulate their conduct; to all intents and purposes this would be something like the state as it currently exists.
- The lack of a centralised justice system would erode the possibility of universal legal norms and thus undermine the rule of law. As a result, unscrupulous individuals might exploit protective associations for their own gain, turning them into 'protection rackets'.
- There is a danger that people would 'free-ride' by taking advantage of the efforts of their neighbours to provide security without paying into the scheme. If widespread, a lack of reciprocity would lead to a breakdown of trust and order.

Still more problematic, however, is that anarcho–capitalism risks creating new concentrations of power based on economic domination: the state would cease to be an interventionist actor, leaving private corporations to fill the void. Left-wing anarchists argue that such a scenario is potentially more damaging than communism, which combines economic and political power in a totalitarian formula. Corporations have only one goal, namely to maximise profits; and without a state to regulate wealth creation, corporate power becomes rapacious.

5 *Collectivist anarchism*

Collectivist anarchists also advocate freedom and self-government, but stress that true freedom and justice can be achieved only through uncoerced cooperation and solidarity. As the Italian anarchist Errico Malatesta (1853–1932) argued:

'The freedom we want… is not an absolute metaphysical, abstract freedom which in practice is inevitably translated into the oppression of the weak; it is real freedom, possible freedom, which is the conscious community of interests, voluntary solidarity.'

5.1 Collectivist anarchism and Marxism

The widely held view that Marxists and collectivist anarchists agree about a common end (a classless, stateless society) but differ about the means to that end is inadequate. At a deeper level, the disagreement is about the nature of the state and its relationship to the economy and society.

Both Marxists and collectivist anarchists view the state as a form of tyranny because it institutionalises the economic and political domination of a ruling class. Through the assertion of political sovereignty, the state enables the ruling class to maintain its power within clearly defined territorial borders, which it achieves by monopolising the means of violence and ideological hegemony.

Like communists, collectivist anarchists see the traditional state as an instrument of class oppression and advocate equality as a necessary condition for the maximum liberty of all; unlike communists, however, they reject Marx's theory of the dictatorship of the proletariat as a transitional government, arguing that even the most enlightened administrators are inevitably corrupted by power.

- For Marxists, the abolition of the state only makes sense as a necessary result of the abolition of social classes, with whose disappearance the need for class domination is eliminated. Marxists (and particularly Marxist–Leninists) believe that the best strategy for winning power is through an organised revolutionary party (the vanguard), led by professional revolutionaries. These professional revolutionaries would then assume responsibility for the moral and political leadership of the new society.
- For collectivist anarchists such as Mikhail Bakunin (1814–76), on the other hand, Marxism simply leads to a dictatorship *over* the proletariat. For Bakunin, the point is not who controls the state but the legitimacy of the state itself as an instrument of domination. All forms of organised political power result in one thing: the domination of man by man, whether or not this domination is in the service of the bourgeoisie or the working class. Bakunin believed that real emancipation could only result from the self-organisation of the people, rather than from the kind of hierarchical leadership characteristic of mass political parties that always results in rule by a few (oligarchy).

Although the arguments of the anarchists proved correct in the Soviet Union, where a new ruling class gradually took control of the state, it is difficult to see how collectivist anarchists would be able to achieve socialism without some form of collective social organisation. Revolution requires leadership, and although Bakunin believed that the last act of the positivist–revolutionary state must be to abolish itself, it is unclear how this would be possible in practice.

5.2 Mutualism

The concept of '**mutualism**' is one of the main ideological innovations of collectivist anarchism, and can be traced back to the radical thinker Proudhon. Although often seen as a utopian socialist, Proudhon was closer to the anarchist tradition as a result of his moralistic notion of freedom as justice and truth. Proudhon believed that the 'greatest amount of freedom coincides with the greatest recognition of right and duty, and the greatest unfreedom with extreme ignorance and corruption'. In this sense, he advocated a qualified form of perfectionism, which entailed the moderation of instinct in favour of virtue, but (unlike Godwin) did not believe in the perfectibility of human nature. Rather, he believed it was essential to restore balance and harmony in man's social and political affairs.

Proudhon rejected Mill's conception of negative freedom, which he saw as a means for justifying possessive individualism and inherited privilege. He argued that 'all property is theft', and that the accumulation of capital violates the principle of balance, and hence results in injustice, inequality and independence. Like the young Marx, he considered the power of capital and the power of the state interdependent. The nation-state provides a sovereign juridical/territorial framework within which a small proper-tied class is able to exploit the labour of the propertyless masses. However, Proudhon argued that, although the modern state is specific to capitalism, i.e. it is dominated by capitalists, it demonstrates a continuity with historic forms of domination.

Note Although Marx was critical of Proudhon's utopianism, there are similarities between their views on the role of the state as a 'parasitic outgrowth' of bourgeois society.

Proudhon conceived of mutualism as a system of *reciprocal exchange*. As a moralist, he believed that, with the expansion of science and morality, society moves hypothetically towards a state of 'moral convergence' in which moral and political questions are resolved through general agreement. According to this view:

rational individuals would no more need to be forced to act in the right manner than they would need to be forced to take account of the laws of physics when building a house.

Bakunin agreed with Proudhon that the power of capital and the power of the state are the same, and that the proletariat could not emancipate itself through the assumption of state power. Unlike Marx, who held that a dictatorship of the proletariat would eventually give way to a classless order, Bakunin the romantic nihilist argued that a post-revolutionary state would simply perpetuate social domination in another form.

However, it was another Russian thinker, Piotr Kropotkin (1842–1921), who attempted to provide a scientific basis for mutualism by using a revised from of Darwinism. In effect, Kropotkin replaced Darwin's emphasis on natural selection through competition with an emphasis on natural selection through *cooperation*. He reasoned that the most successful species are those (such as ants) that work in unison rather than in competition, and that humans must inevitably cooperate if they wish to achieve anything worthwhile.

Russian anarchists also believed fervently in violent struggle against the existing social order, and Bakunin envisaged spontaneous uprisings of the masses (peasants and workers) in widespread insurrections as a result of which the state would be abolished and replaced by autonomous communes on the model of the Paris Commune of 1871. However, revolutionary anarchists became notorious in the 1890s for employing terrorism, and the movement was greatly discredited as a result. One reason for the rise of arbitrary political violence was the incoherence of anarchist politics and a general belief in the utility of shock tactics: violence was seen to have a cleansing effect, an extreme expression of cultural alienation and nihilism. Anarchists received less support than Marxists, who achieved a more advanced form of political organisation. Anarchists operated in small cells, cut off from mainstream society, cultivating an implacable hostility towards bourgeois society.

5.3 Anarcho–syndicalism

One form of collectivist anarchism which did achieve political success is anarcho–syndicalism, which linked revolutionary violence and mass activism. '**Syndicalism**' is derived from the French word for trade union. Anarcho–syndicalists advocate the organisation of exploited groups within democratic associations, and believe that order can be guaranteed through a people's militia rather than hierarchical law enforcement.

Following Georges Sorel (1847–1922), anarcho–syndicalists seek to transform trade unions into revolutionary organisations, making 'syndicates' rather than communes the basic units of a collectivist order. The revolution, if it takes place, should assume the form of a general strike, in the course of which workers take over the means of production and exchange, and abolish the state.

Anarcho–syndicalists focus on projects such as workers' control and the promotion of self-sufficiency, but there is disagreement between ecoanarchists who advocate a **primitivist**, back-to-the-land agenda, and those who see technology as a liberating force. However, all anarcho-syndicalists agree that technology should be adapted to suit human needs rather than commercial interests, and the main object of anarcho–syndicalist attacks is the wasteful consumerism of modern industrial society.

5.4 Problems with collectivist anarchism

For anarchists, all forms of organised authority result in the domination of man by man, whether or not this domination exists in the service of the bourgeoisie or of the proletariat. The state is no more than a concrete political expression of the conflict between rulers and ruled. Anarchists argue that collective emancipation can come about only through the following processes:

- The 'self-abolition' of the state. The final act of the state should be to abolish itself, thereby giving way to the spontaneous self-organisation of the people.
- The introduction of rotating forms of leadership, designed to prevent the re-emergence of a full-time leadership, based on a permanent bureaucratic staff responsible for administering the needs of the community.
- The reorganisation of economic activity into small, autonomous productive units based on democratic supervision and oriented towards local needs.
- A fair division of labour tasks, to ensure that each member of the community shares the burden of stressful and/or strenuous manual work.

While noble in intent, and rational in inspiration, there are problems with systems of this nature, which would be very difficult to organise in the absence of a wider societal collapse, e.g. following a natural disaster or severe energy crisis. The following problems can be identified:

- There is the question of relations between autonomous communities: how would these communities govern their inter-communal affairs without some kind of federal or confederal administrative structure?
- It is difficult to see how collectivist anarchists would be able to achieve a cooperative socialist system without some form of centralised organisation and planning. Marxists argue that without a rational system of resource allocation it is impossible to organise production.
- Despite their emphasis on spontaneous cooperation, collectivist anarchists fail to show how a loose network of autonomous communities could identify and satisfy the changing needs of individuals. Without a market-led or state-led mechanism of resource allocation, there would be no way of predicting and reacting to fluctuations in demand.

6 *Anarchism and the anti-globalisation movement*

The anti-globalisation movement emerged from localised struggles against state violence and neoliberal corruption in the developing world, e.g. the Zapatista movement in Mexico, and the increasing control of politics by corporate elites in the developed world (e.g. leading to the anti-capitalist riots in Seattle in 1999).

Note The protests in Seattle in 1999 were a seminal moment in the emergence of the anti-globalisation movement. Governments have responded to these protests by tightening security and redefining some forms of protest as terrorism.

Although comprising hundreds of small and medium-sized groups pursuing a wide array of agendas, protest groups share a common concern with the social, cultural and environmental impact of neoliberal globalisation. Their principal aim has been to disrupt international economic conferences such as the G20 Summit in London in 2009, to forge networks of opposition to the so-called Washington consensus, and to challenge the hegemonic position of corporate capitalism.

The role played by anarchists in this loose rainbow alliance of protest groups is not immediately clear to outsiders. Media attention is usually fixated on the antics of small groups of anarchists who seek to use violence to disrupt peaceful protests; although exaggerated, there is some truth in this caricature. However, the self-understanding of anarchist groups such as *die Autonomen* (German for 'the autonomous') and *¡Ya basta!* (Spanish for 'Enough already!') is more complex.

At the heart of anti-globalisation campaigns is opposition to the harmful impact of trade liberalisation and finance capitalism on local and regional economies. Unregulated capitalism is seen to usurp power away from people and governments, making it more difficult for communities to engage in sustainable development. Anti-globalisation protesters paint a grim image of corporate finance capitalism as a monolithic machine devouring resources and despoiling the environment in the pursuit of unlimited profits. This highly emotive message has led many traditionally law-fearing communities to engage in activism in the belief that ordinary people can make a difference.

Anarchist participation in such protest movements reflects the renewed appeal of collectivist ideologies of autonomy and democratic self-management after the collapse of Marxism–Leninism. David Miller notes that in the 1960s and 1970s there was an affinity between anarchism and the New Left, with both criticising the banality of life in administered mass societies and the failure of state socialism to offer a viable alternative to capitalism. In the 1990s, a new theme emerged uniting anarchists and anti-capitalists, namely a concern with non-authoritarian, decentralised forms of organisation as alternatives to the capitalist state, and a belief that modern opposition groups could (unlike Leninists) take 'power' without controlling the state.

In addition, many anarchists have been attracted to the anti-globalisation movement precisely because it is a form of political activism. It may seem absurd for affluent Westerners to barricade themselves into buildings and confront the police, but political activism is in many cases its own reward, even at the risk of personal injury. The physicality of the act of rebellion has always attracted radicals, and in an age of deep political apathy and cynicism it is unsurprising that many choose to channel their resentment through violence. However, anarchists can be criticised for engaging in protest for its own sake and for causing disturbances in the full knowledge that protest is unlikely to change anything as real political change typically comes from within the political system itself rather than from outside.

Key terms and concepts

Autonomy	The state of being independent and responsible for one's actions
Egoism	The theory that pursuit of one's own welfare is the highest good
Mutualism	Anarcho–collectivist principle of reciprocity and cooperative labour
Primitivism	Radical branch of ecoanarchism, which advocates a return to pre-industrial human communities
Solidarity	Anarcho–collectivist principle based on the ideal of brotherhood and human cooperation
Syndicalism	Form of radical collectivist organisation based on self-governing associations of workers and peasants
Utopianism	Idealistic political theory that posits an imaginary or perfect society
Voluntarism	Doctrine holding that individuals have an obligation to obey the law because they have given their consent to be ruled

CHAPTER 5 Nationalism

1 Introduction

Nationalism is a core topic in the Edexcel A2 specification, and issues and themes relating to nationalism are also relevant for the AQA and OCR specifications. Students taking the Edexcel exam are strongly advised to cover this topic in detail as it connects with other core topics such as liberalism, conservatism and multiculturalism. In examination questions you are required to show a comprehensive understanding of the progressive and destructive dimensions of nationalism, the difference between statist and cultural nationalism, the links between conservatism, nationalism and imperialism, the connections between nationalism and racialism, and the extent to which nationalism is compatible with liberal political principles.

Given the wide range of historical and contemporary examples from which to choose, the ideological contradictions in nationalism are relatively easy to identify. Yet all too often students' responses contain too much narrative and too little theoretical discussion. For this reason, it is important to focus on the core issues, in particular the function of *sovereignty* in the organisation of nation-states. You must be able to demonstrate an understanding of the advantages and disadvantages of sovereignty, the extent to which the assertion of sovereignty is linked to violence and war, and the limitations of sovereignty as an ordering principle in the global age.

Note You should avoid producing too much historical narrative in your answers. More credit will be given for detailed theoretical analysis backed up by relevant examples.

Unlike socialism or liberalism, nationalism is a political doctrine rather than a coherent ideology in itself. Hence we sometimes speak of 'conservative nationalism' or 'liberal nationalism', concepts that are based on very different views of the nation, the state, patriotism and sovereignty. Some ideologies, such as Marxism, are seen to be inconsistent with nationalism, although history demonstrates the appeal of nationalism for some communist leaders. As a mobilising force, appeals to the nation are more powerful than appeals to class.

Key issues and debates
- the concept of sovereignty;
- the distinction between nations and states;
- the difference between nationalism and racialism;
- state-seeking nationalism and cultural nationalism; and
- progressive and reactionary forms of nationalism.

2 Core ideas of nationalism

2.1 Nations

Nations can be defined as communities of people linked by a shared language, **culture**, religion and traditions. Nations are said to exist where a community of people, united by common experience and common history, feel and articulate an identity of interests between themselves and against outsiders. Social scientists who study nationalism have developed a wide range of models for explaining the phenomenon. One of the principal areas of disagreement concerns the 'modernity' of nations: have nations always existed in some recognisable form or are they a functional political outcome of modernisation processes?

- Cultural anthropologists emphasise the 'primordial' nature of nations, which they argue have their roots in pre-modern ethnic communities. They point to the continuity of ancient civilisations such as Persia and Greece, but they concede that there are major differences between the ancient and modern versions of these civilisations. Anthony D. Smith, author of *Myths and Memories of the Nation*, is representative of this tradition, arguing that nations are versions of historic 'ethnies'.
- Sociologists, on the other hand, emphasise the 'socially constructed' nature of nations. They point to the absence of nationalist movements before the eighteenth century, and argue that nationalism is a political rather than cultural phenomenon. Nationalism, according to Ernest Gellner (1925–95), is a political doctrine based on the principle that the boundaries of the nation and state should coincide. Nationalists promote shared cultural identities through education and citizenship in order to negotiate the economic challenge of industrialisation.

This debate is complex, but we can simplify the problem by comparing nations that have their roots in a distant but recognisable ethnic community, and nations that have their roots in the political and economic revolutions of the past two centuries. The former are based on the endurance of a common ethnicity and civilisation, e.g. China; the latter cohere around a common commitment to statehood, e.g. modern Iraq. The vast majority of nations in the world today belong to the latter category, and cannot be traced back to a single 'essential' source.

National consciousness emerges through the construction of real or imagined common interests and **identities**, a process that may or may not result in the formation of a territorial **nation-state**. Successful nation-states are usually based on the following factors:

- *Language*. Although languages such as English, Spanish and Arabic are international, language is one of the most important aspects of culture. This is because language embodies distinctive attitudes, values, forms of expression and ways of thinking.
- *Religion*: e.g the Shi'ite branch of Islam in Iran and Iraq, or Orthodox Christianity in Greece and Serbia. English nationhood is also connected to the rise of Protestantism as a national religion in the seventeenth century.
- *Shared history*. For nationalists, the cultivation of a shared historical past and shared traditions is essential to the promotion of a shared sense of nationhood. The myth of Joan of Arc in French history is an obvious example.

2.2 Nation-states

Nation-states are the *principal units of political rule* in the modern era, reflecting the enduring appeal of nationalism. The world is divided into more than 170 nation-states, ranging from multi-ethnic federations to ethnically homogeneous island nations. Most nations are based on a unitary state, but many larger nations are organised into federations. Some, such as Norway, are homogeneous; others, such as Russia, contain numerous minorities, who speak Russian but retain their own distinctive cultures.

France is an example of a unitary nation-state based on a dominant national group. France is a highly centralised country, which nevertheless has strong regional dialects and traditions, e.g. Provençal, Breton and Corsican. By contrast, the United Kingdom is a multinational state — a constitutional monarchy in which limited autonomy has been devolved to Scotland, Wales and Northern Ireland.

The boundaries of nation-states are essentially arbitrary, but are typically the outcome of historical struggles between linguistic/religious communities for control over territory. For example, parts of modern-day Spain were once ruled by North African Arabs (the Moors), while the territory of modern-day Poland was divided between Russia, Austria and Prussia until 1920. To a certain extent, the acquisition of statehood is an accident of history and, as Gellner argues, many nations simply do not 'make it': they are either absorbed into larger political entities through war, dynastic succession or revolution, e.g. the fate of Burgundy or Prussia, or they cease to reproduce their distinctive cultures and assimilate into a larger dominant culture, e.g. the fate of Kashubs in Poland or the Sorbs in Germany.

It is important to bear in mind that, while most nationalists aspire to statehood, not *all* forms of nationalism are state-seeking: many cultural nations (such as Wales) do not seek statehood because it makes little sense to do so. Rather, their main aim is to preserve their distinctive cultural traditions, or achieve sub-state rights, within a larger political entity. Many cultural nationalists recognise the advantages their people already have as citizens of an established sovereign state.

2.3 Sovereignty and self-determination

Sovereignty is defined as *supreme or unrestricted power*. In nationalist ideologies, sovereignty is understood as indivisible, although adherence to international treaties and membership of transnational organisations mean that nation-states rarely possess absolute sovereignty over decision-making. It is important to differentiate between:

- the *internal* sovereignty of a government, based on the fact that it is the ultimate authority within the territorial state; and
- the *external* sovereignty of a state, which refers to the independence of nation-states within the international community.

In a geopolitical sense, a sovereign nation is one that is capable of defending its people and territory from incursion by other sovereign states, and recognised as a legitimate territorial entity by other states or international organisations such as the United Nations. As such, sovereignty is seen as a prior condition for self-determination. Whether or not a particular community shares a common culture, the goals of self-determination are always the same: for the community to have control over its own destiny, and for the community to be ruled by individuals who share the interests and identity of the community in question.

A state can be considered sovereign in an external sense even if there is conflict within that state over who actually governs. This is because the principle of national sovereignty is a basic ordering principle of international law, and conflicts within states over who rules become issues of international concern only if those conflicts have implications for regional or international stability, e.g. in the case of civil war in one country drawing in other states. This problem can be seen in the case of Lebanon, where continuing internal conflict has led to repeated foreign interventions.

Nationalists stress the importance of sovereignty for three main reasons:
- Sovereignty is a condition of national independence. The nineteenth and twentieth centuries were dominated by the struggle of different nations for sovereignty, and nationalist mythologies are closely bound up with the idea of patriotic struggle against foreign political oppression.
- Sovereignty is connected to belief in popular government, an idea with its roots in the French Revolution. Before the rise of nationalism, sovereignty was linked to the power of monarchs, whose legitimacy was based on loyalty to the ruling dynasty. In nationalist ideologies, by contrast, sovereignty is seen to reside with the people, whose consent is required in order to govern.

- Nationalists argue that sovereign nations are the logical basis for political organisation because cultural communities have a moral interest in adhering to cultures and sustaining these cultures over time. It is argued that, for nations to express their culture freely, they must be able to determine their own future without interference, and only sovereign statehood can ensure that the national community is represented by leaders who share the interests of the group.

2.4 Race and ethnicity

A nation is a community of people linked by shared language, religion and traditions. A **race**, on the other hand, is a group of people of common ancestry. The latter is, strictly speaking, a biological category. Humans all belong to the same species, *Homo sapiens*. However, as a result of differences in skin pigmentation, eye colour, height and hair texture, people divide the human race into categories such as Caucasian, African or Asian. This reflects the influence of nineteenth-century anthropology, which attached great cultural significance to physical appearance, but it conceals the extent to which physical difference can be traced along a continuum of minor distinctions rather than conformity to ideal racial types.

There is some ambiguity in the use of terms, such as 'ethnic-nation', that reflect the tension between national identity and ethnicity. Many countries are nation-states based on a majority ethnic group, e.g. ethnic Malays in Malaysia. In both cases, the majority group defines itself as the hegemonic 'ethnic-nation', but in neither case is this ethnic-nation synonymous with the nation as a whole. In Malaysia, there are large Chinese and Indian minorities whose physical appearance and culture are distinct, yet who still identify themselves as citizens of Malaysia. Neither consanguinity nor ethnicity constitutes a logical basis for determining national identity: sometimes ethnicity correlates with nationality; more often it does not.

This problem becomes even more apparent in the case of multi-ethnic societies such as South Africa, where the black African majority lives alongside white, Asian and mixed-race groups. This 'rainbow nation', as it was named by Archbishop Desmond Tutu, cannot be defined in racial terms because any attempt at exclusive definition would be quickly exhausted by the wide array of South African identities.

Despite this, the terms 'nation' and 'race' are confused because it is often assumed that culture and citizenship must be linked to ethnicity. **Racialists** in particular believe that the different racial or genetic make-up of human races has significant social and political consequences, but there is evidence to suggest that any culture can be assimilated by a child from any racial group, just as any child can acquire any language when exposed to it.

From this perspective, cultures are based on acquired characteristics, and are not solely dictated by genetic factors. As Gellner argues, humans are unique in the sense that the societies into which they are divided exhibit a variety of behavioural forms, all of which are broadly compatible with our shared genetic inheritance.

Note You must not confuse the terms *nation* and *race*. A nation is a cultural or political entity, while a race is a biological classification.

2.5 Patriotism

Patriotism arouses deep passions and is easily harnessed in pursuit of nationalist goals. The emotive appeal of patriotism allows political leaders to call for unity and sacrifice during times of crisis and war, although in the modern era it is more generally expressed through harmless competitive activities such as sport. Patriotism is not the same thing as nationalism, however: patriotism implies a positive identification with the civic and political traditions of a country, rather than attachment to a culture or ethnicity. As such it is championed by liberals who dislike the darker overtones of nationalism.

Nationalists emphasise 'love of country' as the highest political virtue because membership of a state is linked to positive identification with its history and traditions, as well as a defence of its future interests. Professor Maurizio Viroli defines patriotism in constitutional terms as the 'affection that a people feel for their country understood not as native soil, but as a community of free men living together for the common good'.

As Professor Chaim Gans argues, however, this republican definition of patriotism excludes the cultural dimension of citizenship in nation-states. Is it possible, he asks, for citizens to identify with their country in purely civic or political terms? Or is loyalty to a state not founded on culture and ethnicity?

This problem goes to the heart of the debate on nationalism in modern political theory, and reveals the level of disagreement between those who see nationalism as a primarily cultural force, and those who see it as a political movement. The civic definition of patriotism implies that it is possible to explain loyalty to the state in purely political terms, but the evidence suggests that patriotism is normally based on more emotive forces than identification with constitutional norms.

Civic identity may be a *necessary* component of patriotism, but it is unlikely to be a *sufficient* condition of belonging in and of itself. Nationalism is, however, more often than not based on a defence of identity and the exclusion of 'unassimilable' minorities.

2.6 Identity and exclusion

Over and above civic and political factors, nationalists also emphasise the distinctiveness and boundaries of their specific community, whether these are defined in terms of language, culture, religion or other criteria. Conservative nationalists in particular assert the ideal of an 'organic community', based on the view that mankind is naturally divided into distinct ethno–linguistic groups, each of which possesses a unique or irreducible identity. Identity is derived not just from socialisation into the norms and practices of the group, but from a sense of being different or unique.

This creates a sense of exclusiveness — an indefinable quality of belonging, which presupposes the exclusion of out-groups. For nationalists, the historical emergence of nations is a process of cultural transformation based on *closure*. This functions by presenting the national group as a distinct cultural and territorial unit within clearly defined borders demarcating two categories of individuals:

* the homogeneous domestic realm of the national group ('us'); and
* the heterogeneous external realm ('them').

In other words, closure involves the reinforcement of identity through the exclusion of non-members.

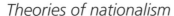

Exclusion may work in different ways, but it is usually practised at the expense of ethnic or linguistic minorities. In its most extreme forms (as in South Africa under Apartheid), it can be used to exclude a majority of the population by denying them full political rights or limiting their freedom of movement. Although black South Africans outnumbered white South Africans by five to one, they remained excluded from white definitions of the nation, and were thus denied the right to democratic representation (unlike mixed-race 'coloureds' who were given limited rights).

3   Theories of nationalism

Political theorists traditionally distinguish between a *civic* form of nationalism based on political association, and an *ethnic* form of nationalism based on common descent. Thinkers such as Hans Kohn, author of *The Idea of Nationalism*, contrast the 'progressive' civic nationalism typical of Western Europe with the 'reactionary' ethnic nationalism found in Eastern Europe. For Kohn, the difference between civic and ethnic nationalism reflects the uneven political and economic development of the Continent in the eighteenth and nineteenth centuries.

In countries such as England and France, old dynastic loyalties gave way in the seventeenth and eighteenth centuries to a new civic nationalism based on popular sovereignty. Centred on the national bourgeoisie, territorial-civic nationalism implies a commitment to liberal political principles and the development of civil society: the nation is understood as sovereign, while government reflects the will of the people because the individuals who comprise it *volunteer* their consent to be governed. This type of nationalism is seen to be consistent with the atomistic view of society in liberal ideologies, where 'society' is understood as an aggregation of individuals rather than as an identity-based, exclusive community.

Against this type of nationalism Kohn stressed the primordial character of ethnic and cultural nationalism in Eastern Europe. As a result of retarded economic development, nationalism in this multi-ethnic region is typically expressed in terms of identity rather than commitment to civic or political ideals. This reflects a difference in socio-historical development. Whereas the bourgeoisie in Western Europe traditionally understood itself as a 'universal' social class — transcending narrow social categories such as ethnicity — the intelligentsia in Eastern Europe was concerned with defending local identities by emphasising the myth of common descent.

Although this typology remains in use in many textbooks, it is problematic because it ignores the role of cultural factors in state-seeking nationalist movements. It also implies that nationalism in its 'rational' Western form is expressed in purely idealistic terms, emptied of passion and emotion. This fails to take into account the *deliberate cultivation of shared cultural identities* in countries such as England and France, where nationality runs much deeper than commitment to constitutional values.

3.1 State-seeking and cultural nationalism

A more plausible strategy is to distinguish not between civic and ethnic nationalisms (which overlap), but between *cultural* nationalism (where individuals share a moral interest in sustaining their cultures over time) and *state-seeking* nationalism (where states have an interest in their citizens acquiring a common cultural identity, normally for the purposes of economic development).

State-seeking nationalism occurs where states, in pursuit of democracy, economic modernisation or social justice, seek to promote a homogeneous national culture in order to unify the community behind their goals. State-seeking nationalism draws on specific customs and traditions, but the goals in question are essentially political in form and independent of that culture, with culture acquiring an 'instrumental' function, namely for promoting social and political integration. One of the primary mechanisms of cultural homogenisation is the emergence of national education systems.

Cultural nationalism, on the other hand, is based on the politicisation of cultural and linguistic ties that bind particular communities. For cultural nationalists, members of national groups that share a common ancestry have a moral interest in adhering to their culture and in passing on this culture to the next generation. Many forms of cultural nationalism are non-state-seeking because the acquisition of statehood is not always necessary for the preservation of culture.

Most forms of nationalism include both statist and cultural features. Statist nationalism entails a definite cultural dimension because it seeks to promote cultural homogeneity as a means for realising political and economic goals. Cultural nationalism, by contrast, involves a definite political dimension because it seeks to use the state as a means of sustaining and promoting national cultures.

Cultural nationalism is sometimes seen as dangerous because it is based on 'instinctive allegiance' rather than 'considered solidarity'. Yet both cultural and political nationalism can be progressive or reactionary and there are numerous examples of illiberal state-seeking nationalisms where dominant groups employ force to assert their hegemony over minority groups or outsiders.

Note For state-seeking nationalists, culture is a means of *creating* a modern nation-state; for cultural nationalists, the state is a means of *preserving* a historic national culture over time.

3.2 Nationalism, industrialisation and state formation

For modernists such as Gellner, the bourgeoisie represents the historic force behind nationalism as its interests are coterminous with those of the nation itself. Unlike the aristocracy, the bourgeoisie has an interest in promoting national development as a means of achieving hegemony, and it is better placed to provide cultural and economic leadership:

- On the one hand, the bourgeoisie has an interest in economic development, which can be realised only within the context of a unified domestic market. It is for this reason that nationalism and industrialisation coincide, based on the rise of a commercial class committed to economic modernisation.
- On the other hand, the bourgeoisie has an interest in cultural progress, which can be realised only through the growth of literacy, education and communications. For writers on nationalism such as Benedict Anderson, the emergence of 'print capitalism' based on publication of books in the vernacular is a vital element in the process of state formation.

In state-centred nationalism it is national elites themselves who take communities and turn them into nations, by homogenising a variety of local cultures into a distinctive unified society. As Gellner argues, it is nationalism that engenders nations, not

the other way around. This process reflects the need to create stable communities capable of adapting to the needs of rapid economic development in the transition to capitalism. The nation-state represents the ideal political unit within which to organise a modern economy and to sustain industrialisation.

The reason for this is important: whereas pre-industrial states tend to have a fixed social structure, industrial societies must continually change in order to compete. Economic development requires not only free markets, but also literacy, mobility and communications, which are impossible in traditional agrarian societies where traditional elites rule over a static peasant population with its own local cultures and traditions. As the requirements of development increase, there is a growing need to homogenise these local customs and practices in the interests of economic efficiency and rationality. This process involves:

- The codification of a national language from a variety of local dialects. Only if all members of a population can understand each other is it possible for a national culture to emerge.
- New methods of socialisation. For example, national education systems promote literacy, as well as creating a state-driven identity as each generation is taught a common history and shared set of values.
- The creation of stable territorial boundaries, without which a nation cannot assert its sovereignty, and without sovereignty it is vulnerable to external interference.
- The cultivation of national myths. All cultures possess a mythology that helps to sustain group identity and cohesiveness.

To summarise: although nationalists draw on pre-existing ethnic and cultural identities in the process of state formation, the real dynamic of state seeking nationalism is the homogenisation of culture in the interests of modernisation. This normally coincides with the interests of political and economic elites who seek to compete with other nation-states in the struggle for territory and resources.

4 *Liberal nationalism*

The rise of nationalism is closely associated with European history, although it is important to avoid an overly Eurocentric approach. The first truly 'modern' nation was France, but as Benedict Anderson has shown, nationalism was already an emergent force in the Spanish-speaking colonies of South America *before* the French Revolution.

Although it is simplistic to argue that 'Western' nationalism is purely state-centred (and thus progressive), while 'Eastern' nationalism is exclusively cultural (and therefore unprogressive), it is possible to identify a *liberal* form of nationalism in which the nation is understood as a 'moral entity' uniting the citizens of a given nation-state on the basis of universal rights and freedoms. For liberal nationalists the nation embodies the ideals of sovereignty, **self-determination** and citizenship, implying a progressive commitment to national sovereignty as the basis of political legitimacy.

4.1 The nation as 'moral entity'

Liberals see nations as moral entities that unite the citizens of different communities not only in terms of shared culture, but on the basis of universal rights and freedoms. Liberal nationalism can be seen as a progressive doctrine, which bridged the transition from the age of absolutism to the modern era of nation-states. Before the rise of nationalism, loyalty to the state was defined in terms of loyalty to the monarchy, but in the eighteenth century 'crown-centred nationalism' gave way to a new belief in popular sovereignty. According to this doctrine, sovereignty resides not in the monarchy or the state, but in the nation as a body of citizens. The French Revolution established two principles:

- the universal ideals of liberty, equality and fraternity, which form the basis of the modern ideal of citizenship; and
- the right of all peoples to self-determination.

It is these principles that led to the rise of nationalism and state-building in nineteenth-century Europe. Inspired by the French example, nationalists in German and Italian lands, in Hungary, Greece, Poland and elsewhere, set in motion a process of national mobilisation that had three distinct aims: to rid their countries of foreign interference; to establish sovereign jurisdiction over all the members of the ethnic–linguistic group; and to mobilise the 'national' community behind the cultural and political ideals of the ruling class, promoting a new state-driven identity.

Nationalism in this form has a strong appeal because nationalist leaders are able, through the ideal of the nation, to identify themselves with the destiny and culture of their people. By linking the nation's future with some glorious past, nationalists promote an idealised (but powerful) vision of the benefits of sovereignty and self-determination. This can be seen in two examples:

- The Risorgimento in nineteenth-century Italy, which led to the unification of the Italian states into a single nation-state with its capital in Rome. Although Italian unification was a product of diplomacy and war, the new rulers owed much to the resurrection of traditional myths surrounding the glory of Rome and the achievements of Italian culture. This laid the basis for the emergence of 'Liberal Italy', based on the hegemony of the new national bourgeoisie and the belated economic development of the peninsula.
- During the final decades of the Austro-Hungarian Empire, Czech nationalism was directed against the dominance of German-speakers who had ruled the region for centuries. The First World War led to the final collapse of the *ancien régime* in central Europe, creating several states that had not previously existed. The creation of Czechoslovakia unified Bohemia, Moravia, Slovakia and Ruthenia under the liberal leadership of Thomas Masaryk, who sought to promote *national* political development without harming the *multinational* character of the new state. However, the presence of a large German minority in the Sudetenland made it impossible for the Czechs to assert their sovereignty, and the state was dismembered by Daladier, Chamberlain, Mussolini and Hitler following the Munich Agreement of 1938.

Liberalism and nationalism are compatible where the rights and freedoms of constituent groups are protected, where individuals are allowed to pursue their legitimate interests unconstrained, and where private property is protected in law. Liberal nationalists place a strong emphasis on constitutional mechanisms for protecting civic freedoms, while promoting assimilation with the core values of the state. Yet, as George Schöpflin, author of *Nationalism and Ethnicity in Europe*, argues, even in Western Europe, national identity is still rooted in a shared ethnicity that is essential for cultural reproduction. Although liberal nationalism is progressive, the nation-building is also based on exclusion and intolerance.

4.2 The ambivalence of English nationalism

The ambivalence of English nationalism is exemplified by the political exclusion of Catholics in Britain until the turn of the twentieth century and the assertion of English national identity over the 'Celtic fringe' of the British Isles. England was a separate kingdom until the later Tudor period when it developed into a centralised state based on a unified political administration. The formation of the United Kingdom dates back to the Act of Union with Scotland (1707) and Ireland (1801).

The ascendancy of England was a result of the formation of a stable and territorially secure English state, which was used to form the foundations of a *multinational dynastic agglomeration*. After subduing the Scottish Highlanders and colonising Ireland, the extension of rule from London was a logical consequence of the hegemony of the English and the expansion of English imperial power overseas.

Krishan Kumar, author of *The Making of English National Identity*, argues that, although committed to rational ideals, English nationalism developed as an imperial or 'missionary' function based on the 'attachment of a dominant or core ethnic group to a state entity that conceives itself as dedicated to some large cause or purpose, religious, cultural or political'. He argues that the ambivalence of English nationalism, and the confusion of England with Britain, can be resolved by seeing English national identity as the nationalism of a *conservative–imperial state*. Kumar analyses England's conservative–imperial past in terms of two empires:
- the *internal* empire (the United Kingdom), based on the subjugation of the Scots, Welsh and Irish and their total loss of sovereignty; and
- the *external* empire (the British Empire), based on the subjugation of parts of Asia, Africa and the Middle East (regions that regained sovereignty only after 1945, following the rise of anti-colonial nationalist movements opposed to European rule).

In modern times it has become fashionable to speak of British rather than English nationhood. 'Britishness' appears to offer a more inclusive, civic conception of identity than 'Englishness', which has stronger ethnic overtones. However, the idea of Englishness remains powerful and has gained traction in recent years. This correlates with the parallel development of national consciousness in Wales and Scotland as more people have come to question the purpose of the United Kingdom. This does not mean the UK is in danger of breaking up as both left-wing and right-wing critics often suggest; but it does indicate that the constituent nations of the UK increasingly identify with their own nation first, and Britain second.

5   *Conservative nationalism*

Conservatives embrace nationalism because the nation embodies tradition and shared cultural identity. Conservatives define the nation in an essentialist form as an 'organic community', which imposes unconditional obligations on individuals based on *instinctive allegiance*. Conservative nationalism can be traced back to the philosophical romanticism of the German counter-Enlightenment — an ideological reaction against Enlightenment rationalism and the 'excesses' of the French Revolution.

5.1 Holism and political romanticism

Professor Elie Kedourie (1926–92) suggested that this type of nationalism is based on a 'holistic' reaction to the Kantian equation of virtue and free will. According to Immanuel Kant, all individuals have an obligation to strive for self-determination, and all forms of political association should reflect the autonomous sovereign will of citizens (who in return incur an obligation to recognise and obey public authority).

Note It is important to note the links between conservative nationalism and the traditional conservative belief in an 'organic community' that is culturally exclusive and places specific obligations on its members.

For thinkers such as Johann Fichte (1762–1814) and Johann Herder (1744–1803), however, this view contradicts the origin of apparently 'autonomous' identities in pre-existing 'organic wholes':

The whole is *always* greater than the sum of its parts: individuals derive their identity and purpose by participating in culture, assimilation into which is non-negotiable.

At the same time language provides the essential medium for the historical evolution of cultures, making possible the emergence and communication of shared norms and values.

For conservative–romantic nationalists, the diversity of cultures must be defended against the rationalising, universalising imperative of Enlightenment rationalism, which seeks to 'level' or extinguish pre-modern beliefs and irrational attachments in the name of Reason. The disruption of traditional historical identities can be prevented only by resisting this powerful dynamic, which German idealists associated directly with English mercantilism and French rationalism.

George Mosse, author of *The Crisis of German Ideology*, argued that the political consequence of this romantic defence of 'authentic identity' can be seen in the rise of German *völkish* nationalism in the nineteenth century, which contributed to (but did not directly cause) the development of National Socialism in the 1920s. Conservative–romantic nationalists take seriously the nationalist commitment to self-determination, but seek to replace considered solidarity with instinctual allegiance within an organic national community.

5.2 Conservative nationalism and the German Empire, 1871–1914

The development of nationalism in Wilhelmine Germany provides an excellent example of the ideological impact of romanticism on politics. Germany was not the only country to develop a reactionary form of nationalism, but the rapid rise of the German lands from a patchwork of principalities and kingdoms in the early nineteenth century to a powerful industrial giant in the early twentieth century led to an acceleration of nationalist and imperialist aspirations among the German bourgeoisie.

Although the cultural force behind German nationalism was the liberal bourgeoisie, the real motor of German unity was the Prussian leader, Otto von Bismarck, whose primary aim was to weaken the influence of (Catholic) Austria in German affairs, and to challenge the power of France. Liberal nationalists had hoped to steer Bismarck towards support for a constitutional monarchy, but his primary loyalty was to the King of Prussia, who was crowned German Emperor in 1871.

The decline of liberal nationalism in Germany was a product of several developments, the most important of which include:

- The policies of agrarian and industrial elites, who sought to use the state as a vehicle for promoting German economic influence abroad.
- The social conservatism of the ruling class, which was disinterested in political reform or universal ideals of liberalism, and which saw the unified nation-state as a means for defending the existing social order.
- The desire to become an imperial power and compete with Britain, France and Russia for colonial possessions.
- The increasing popularity of xenophobic and anti-Semitic ideas among the German middle classes.

The negative consequences of this transition to conservative nationalism are well known. Germany challenged Franco-British hegemony, demanding an increased sphere of military–political power to match its economic strength. After Bismarck had unified the German states, he abandoned his liberal allies in parliament in favour of an alliance of conservative agrarian and industrial interests. These interests influenced his less cautious successors, who used nationalism as a means for uniting the Germans behind the expansionist goals of the elite, and the aggressive nature of German foreign policy after 1890 contributed to the outbreak of the First World War.

6   *Integral nationalism*

Integral nationalism is a feature of established rather than emerging nations, and represents a logical continuation of conservative–imperial nationalist traditions. Integral nationalists emphasise not simply loyalty and duty to the state, but also the defence of the 'body politic' against alien influences. Integral nationalism is motivated by chauvinistic political goals and neo-Darwinist theories concerning the 'health of the nation'.

In the late nineteenth century, the established powers (Britain, France, Russia and Germany) employed conservative–imperialist nationalism to justify imperial expansion abroad and social integration at home.

In the colonial context, the racial 'superiority' of Europeans became one of the core legitimating ideals of imperialist ideology, emphasising the superiority of the white nations over the darker-skinned peoples of Africa and Asia. European imperialists claimed a right to world leadership on the basis that the European countries were more advanced and could therefore contend they were engaged in a civilising mission to 'educate' the darker-skinned races of the world.

Within Europe itself, however, colonial racism was overshadowed by a new form of 'class racism' directed against workers, who were increasingly seen as the 'dangerous classes' living in the midst of bourgeois civilisation. Not only were workers seen as potentially disloyal in their allegiance to socialist **internationalism**, but they were also seen as a demographic threat to civil society. This was particularly the case in the French Third Republic, after the catastrophic experience of the Paris Commune of 1871, when workers temporarily took control of the French capital.

The dynamics of integral nationalism lie in the cultivation of state patriotism based on the homogenisation of national identity. In contrast with liberal nationalism, integral nationalism belongs to the second phase of state formation in modern Europe (1870–1918). The most powerful example of this phenomenon is Action Française in France, a monarchist movement which called for a return to dynastic leadership and authoritarianism, and whose xenophobic nationalism and anti-Semitism were fuelled by the Dreyfus affair (a political scandal caused by the wrongful conviction of a Jewish-French officer for treason).

Integral nationalism developed into a state ideology, and marked a new phase in the evolution of the modern nation-state. Integral nationalists widened their support in Europe and America, and some of their ideas contributed to revolutionary conservatism and fascism in the inter-war period. Some of their ideas also reappear in neoconservative and communitarian ideologies of authority and identity, where particular stress is placed on the defence of national character against the 'harmful' effects of multiculturalism and immigration.

7 Fascism

The continuity of reactionary nationalism in European political culture can be seen in the rise of fascism in the 1920s. Fascism is a right-wing ideology, which holds that morality is ultimately tied to blood and race, understood in terms of descent and genetic inheritance. Fascists reject the liberal conception of limited government based on constitutionalism and consent, and stress instead the role of *irrational* forces in the determination of political action.

7.1 Militant nationalism

Fascists glorify duty to the nation as the *highest political virtue*. In fascist ideology the nation is understood in racial or ethnic terms as an exclusive unit, which is morally and politically superior to the individuals who comprise it. At the heart of fascist ideology is a concern with the expansion and improvement of the 'race-nation', and with the assimilation or extermination of competing identities deemed inconsistent with the interests of this core ethnic group. For this reason fascist nationalism is opposed to liberal conceptions of citizenship.

Unlike classical nationalism, which asserts that the boundaries of the nation and the state should coincide, fascist nationalism is an expansionist political doctrine based on a social Darwinist belief in the perpetual struggle of nations for survival.

Although the fascist concept of nationhood is based on instinctive allegiance rather than considered solidarity, fascism also draws on a different nationalist tradition, which can be traced back to thinkers such as Rousseau who attacked traditional liberal concepts of democracy, emphasising instead a collectivist vision of the 'general will'.

Rousseau maintained that modern states fail to create a sense of national unity because they do not articulate an *active concept of citizenship*. Although he believed in social equality, Rousseau's critique of bourgeois civilisation and defence of popular sovereignty have encouraged numerous utopian visions of harmonious unified society, including national syndicalism and fascism.

From an authoritarian–collectivist perspective, fascist ideologists hold that bourgeois society is too atomised and individualistic to provide an adequate focal point for mobilising the nation. This perception is reflected in their desire to abolish the distinction between private and public life, and to promote patriotism and complete subservience to the state.

The paradox of fascist nationalism is that it provides an unstable basis for political organisation. By creating unrealistic expectations of national glory and imperialist expansion, fascism fails to establish a basis for the construction of durable political structures. Once fascist leaders embark on a project of expansion without reason, they are forced to divert resources away from national reconstruction towards destructive military campaigns.

7.2 Racialism

Not all fascist ideologies are explicitly racialist, but most fascists adopt a chauvinistic or jingoistic attitude towards other national groups, based either on racialist or culturalist assumptions. Although Italian fascism was primarily concerned with political goals, and introduced anti-Semitic race laws only in 1938, many Italian fascists regarded Africans as inferior to Europeans, which helped to justify Mussolini's expansionist policy in Libya and Abyssinia.

Racialists believe that the racial and genetic character of human 'races' has important social, political and cultural consequences. Racialism was a feature of European imperialist ideologies in the colonial era, and theories of white racial supremacy were developed by a number of European thinkers, including Arthur de Gobineau (1816–82) and Houston Stewart Chamberlain (1855–1939). These thinkers were concerned with what they perceived to be the superior character of the 'Nordic races'. At the root of their ideology was a belief that the Celtic, Germanic and Nordic peoples represent a kind of 'elite' in the hierarchy of races, and must preserve and defend their racial inheritance against dilution from 'inferior' racial groups.

The ideological justification for this belief was found in the assumption that all civilisations must be judged by their cultural and technical achievements. Accordingly, evidence for the racial superiority of the Germanic and Nordic peoples was located in the cultural, scientific and economic sophistication of the Europeans in comparison with the less 'advanced' achievements of the Slavonic, Arabic and African nations. In this way a racialist mythology was created, which became a convenient resource in the process of colonial conquest. Although expressed in less explicit terms, European colonists justified their territorial acquisition and exploitation as an unfortunate but necessary consequence of the attempt to 'civilise' the non-white races of the world, leading to the popular myth of the 'white man's burden' and the necessity of empire.

Within certain fascist ideologies, there is an explicit attempt to justify the racial superiority of the European peoples against the 'racial contamination' of non-European peoples. This was expressed most forcefully in the anti-Semitic ideology of National Socialism, which linked the future of the 'Aryan' people to the destruction of the Jewish race and the colonisation of territory in Eastern Europe. However, in their attempt to 'purify' the German nation, the Nazis not only exterminated the European Jews, but also attempted to eliminate homosexuals, the mentally ill, the disabled, and other groups considered 'unworthy of human life'.

Note In Nazi ideology, the Aryan people are seen as the fair-skinned nations of north-west Europe, racially and culturally distinct from Southern and Eastern European people.

8 Anti-colonial nationalism

The Second World War led to the decline of the European empires in Asia and Africa, and leaders of the **anti-colonial** liberation movements identified with nationalism as a means for achieving political autonomy and economic modernisation. For modernists such as Breuilly, Gellner and Anderson, the emergence of new nation-states in the post-war period is evidence of the essential *modernity* and constructed nature of nationalism: in the aftermath of colonialism, new nations appeared that had never existed before, usually based on more than one constituent ethnic group. Nationalist leaders set about using culture as a means to promote a modern nation-state.

Where national leaders could appeal to historic identities to legitimise their goals, this process was more successful. Where such historic identities were absent, leaders were forced to seek alternative means of legitimation such as Marxism. This is why many post-colonial regimes adopted socialist or communist policies. To understand anti-colonial nationalism it is essential to recognise two distinct ideological trends:

- Adaptation of indigenous non-European intellectuals to the original principles of classical European nationalism, e.g. popular sovereignty and self-determination.
- Rejection of capitalism as an exploitative Western economic system, which was responsible for colonialism and the degradation of indigenous cultures.

Following the example of Lenin, the goal of anti-colonial nationalists was to use the state as an instrument of economic and social change — to accelerate social, economic and cultural development and to impose their own vision of modernity on their people without Western interference. This dynamic may be seen in three examples.

In Algeria the resistance of the Arab nationalist FLN (National Liberation Front) sought to bring to an end 120 years of French rule. Although the French never conceded defeat (their army employed vicious counter-insurgency techniques), they lost the propaganda war and General de Gaulle took the decision to withdraw from North Africa in the 1960s. The FLN combined Arab nationalism with socialism, believing that Algeria could achieve modernisation more effectively as an independent state than as part of France. However, Algeria's leaders have not succeeded in uniting the country's various ethnic groups behind the regime, and, like many countries in Africa, the state is paralysed by corruption and violence.

In the case of Vietnam, the nationalist movement led by Ho Chi Minh was also directed against the French, but also, later, against the USA which believed that the growth of communism in south-east Asia would create a 'domino effect', leading to the loss of other client states in the region to Chinese or Soviet influence. The liberation ideology of the North Vietnamese was bolstered not only by Soviet support, but also by the student movement in the West, which was deeply critical of US foreign policy.

Note Ironically, many anti-colonial nationalists such as Ho Chi Minh were educated in Europe, where they were exposed to European nationalist ideology, which they subsequently deployed against the colonial powers themselves.

Post-colonial Cuba also combined anti-colonial ideology and socialism in a unique form, directed first against the Spanish and then against the USA, which turned Cuba into a quasi-colony in 1898. Employing partisan warfare, and supported by the Soviet Union, Cuban revolutionaries removed the corrupt government of Fulgencio Batista (1901–73) in 1959, and installed the first socialist regime in the Americas since the

Mexican revolution. This led to repeated attempts by the USA to reassert its hegemony over the island nation, including the abortive Bay of Pigs invasion of 1961.

9 Post-communist nationalism

Post-communist nationalism is a feature of the 1990s, following disintegration of the Soviet Union and Yugoslavia. Both countries had attempted to resolve the problems characteristic of multi-ethnic nations by combining socialism with **federalism**. However, in both cases the state was dominated by the leaders of the largest ethnic group — the Russians in the USSR and the Serbs in Yugoslavia. The collapse of Marxism–Leninism led to an explosion of ethnic conflict throughout Eastern Europe, the Caucasus and the Balkans, leading most tragically to the use of genocidal tactics in Bosnia-Herzegovina.

After the death in 1980 of Marshal Tito, who had tried to overcome nationalist conflict through federalism and market socialism, the leaders of the different national groups within federal Yugoslavia began to challenge the political status quo. As the most numerous national group after the Serbs (Orthodox Christians), the Croats (Roman Catholics) wanted to achieve greater autonomy in governing their own affairs, which inevitably antagonised the Serbs who were spread all over the country. The problem lay in the fact that many Serbs lived in the southern borderlands (Kraijina) of Croatia, and these communities faced being cut off geographically from Serbia.

As with Germany after Versailles, Serb nationalists could not accept that fellow Serbs might be subject to foreign rule — particularly in Croatia where so many Serbs had died at the hands of the fascist Ustaše in the Second World War. This led the Serbs to launch the powerful Yugoslav army against Croatia, but it did not prevent Croat nationalists from expelling many Serbs from the Kraijina region.

After this the Bosnians (predominantly Muslims) declared independence, supported by the West and many Arab countries. The Serbs were content to see parts of Bosnia become independent, but not those parts inhabited by ethnic Serbs. As a result, they decided to prevent this loss of territory and population by creating an ethnically pure micro-state called Republika Srpska. This resulted in the use of '**ethnic cleansing**' aimed at eliminating Bosnian Muslim communities in the region. Only when the Serbs threatened the Albanians of Kosovo with a similar fate did the international community act to prevent further ethnic cleansing, leading to the attack on Serbia by NATO forces in 1999. The war led to the fall of Slobodan Milošević, and his arrest and prosecution before the International Criminal Tribunal in The Hague.

Having failed to create a durable constitutional framework for managing nationalist and inter-communal rivalries, Yugoslavia collapsed, leading to the political destabilisation of south-east Europe and a dramatic rise in transnational organised crime. Paradoxically, this negative outcome was partly caused by the Europeans' misguided imposition of sanctions against Serbia in 1992, which encouraged criminals within local elites to develop their own private armies to take advantage of the collapse, many of which became involved in the war itself.

10 Progressive and regressive dimensions of nationalism

The above examples demonstrate the variety of nationalist ideologies, but how can we differentiate between the progressive and destructive aspects of nationalism?

State-centred nationalism is typically seen as progressive because it seeks to create a political framework for economic and cultural modernisation.

Opponents of ethno–cultural nationalism, on the other hand, insist that it is a reactionary and destructive force because it is exclusively concerned with the defence of historic identities rather than with the promotion of modern social and political forms.

Although the Yugoslav example would seem to exemplify this charge, it is not entirely fair as it ignores the normative justification for cultural nationalism based on the assumption that individuals have a legitimate interest in adhering to components of their culture.

The first point to stress is that the principle of sovereignty has both positive and negative implications:

- Sovereignty enables national groups to achieve self-determination, which is essential for the community to express its culture and to determine its own destiny without interference. As a condition of self-determination, sovereignty has emerged as the one of the basic regulating principles of international relations by creating a normative standard for the independence and integrity of national communities.
- Sovereignty's darker side is that it also creates a situation where powerful elites can dominate the population and resources under their jurisdiction — as is the case with integral nationalism and fascism. Critics of sovereignty argue that the state serves to unite one 'national' group for the purpose of enslaving other, weaker groups. Furthermore, sovereign states offer protection exclusively to their own citizens, and recognise human rights only within the confines of their own boundaries.

A second key point is the question of national identity. The promotion of a distinctive national identity is an important feature of all nationalist movements, and has both positive and negative consequences:

- On the one hand, sharing a common identity allows a community to realise its goals more easily in the knowledge that it is working together as a group. This facilitates the development of citizenship and impersonal norms (e.g. trust), which help to sustain the possibility of mutual endeavour, and provide a source of social cohesion.
- On the other hand, nationalism is hostile to cosmopolitanism and multiculturalism. In effect, the state governs in the name of the people as defined in ethnic or cultural terms. As a result, democratic participation and protection under the law are in many instances offered only to members of the core national group, creating social exclusion and conflict.

By establishing the principles of sovereignty and self-determination, the liberal ideals of nationalism contain a commitment to democracy and justice, but these ideas have not always survived intact. In countries such as Italy and Germany, liberal nationalism was ultimately transcended by a more aggressive nationalist ideology, laying the foundations for the rise of fascism.

Nationalism remains an important feature of contemporary political reality and shows few signs of disappearing. The nation remains the primary focus of politics, and the nation-state is still the most successful and enduring model of political organisation in the modern age, even though **globalisation** has reduced the capacity of individual nations to resist a dilution of sovereignty.

Although some politicians still view sovereignty as indivisible, only a handful of states, e.g. the USA and China, have the strategic power to act autonomously and resist outside pressures. Medium-sized nations such as Britain, France and Germany are now all firmly integrated into the EU, a **supra-governmental organisation** that transcends the traditional category of national sovereignty.

The principal threats to national sovereignty arise from:

- Global market forces: no country is immune from pressures arising from the international economy. World trade means that all the major economies are increasingly interdependent.
- International treaties and conventions, which mean that nations have an obligation to follow guidelines or adopt policies that reduce their autonomy.
- Supra-governmental organisations such as the EU, which mean that countries such as Britain increasingly coordinate decision-making with other member states.

Key terms and concepts

Anti-colonialism	Collective name for the different nationalist movements that arose in the twentieth century in opposition to European imperialism
Culture	The distinctive customs, values and achievements that characterise different national groups
Ethnic cleansing	Localised genocide: the attempt to expel or exterminate members of a specific ethnic group from a given territory
Federalism	System of government in which states pool their sovereignty to form a central political unity, but retain autonomy over their own internal affairs
Globalisation	The integration of the world economy into a single global market
Identity	The unchanging qualities and features that characterise different individuals and ethno–cultural groups
Internationalism	Socialist/anarchist belief in the community of interests that exists between nations
National self-determination	Where a national group has control over its own destiny, and is ruled by individuals who share the interests and identity of the group
Nation-state	The principal unit of political rule in the modern era, based on the doctrine that the boundaries of nations and states should coincide
Patriotism	Pride in and attachment to the traditions and culture of one's country
Race	Any of the major subdivisions of mankind, which possess a distinctive physical appearance and/or ethnic identity
Racialism	Theory that different racial groups possess inherited genetic characteristics that make them superior or inferior and have significant social and political consequences
Sovereignty	Supreme authority; the absolute and independent authority of a state within the international community
Supra-governmental organisations	Political bodies such as the EU, which have power or influence transcending national boundaries, governments and institutions

CHAPTER 6 Fascism

1 Introduction

Fascism is a core topic in Unit 3B of the AQA Government and Politics specification. Of all the ideologies studied at A2, fascism demands the highest level of historical knowledge. However, the emphasis is less on comparative historical analysis than on the *generic* and *specific* features of fascist ideologies. Examiners are particularly interested in assessing students' knowledge and understanding of the intellectual, cultural and socio–political context of fascist ideologies, and how these have emerged in opposition to mainstream liberal and conservative ideologies.

Note You must be aware of the generic and specific features of fascist ideologies.

Fascism is a right-wing nationalist ideology, which holds that morality is ultimately tied to blood and race. In fascist ideology, nationality is understood in terms of descent rather than citizenship. While fascists glorify the ethnic 'race-nation', in practice fascist nationalism is reactionary and expansionist, exceeding the traditional nationalist concern with sovereignty and self-determination. For this reason, fascism cannot simply be reduced to nationalism — any more than conservatism can be reduced to traditionalism.

Fascists reject the liberal concept of limited government based on constitutionalism and consent, and assert instead an activist view of politics based on a belief in 'will to power'. In this respect, fascist ideologies are understood as a 'revolt against reason': by rejecting the legal–rational basis of political pluralism, fascist ideologies stress the role of *irrational* forces in the determination of social and political action.

Key issues and debates
- the link between fascism and irrationalism;
- the link between fascism and totalitarianism;
- fascism and populism;
- fascism, nationalism and imperialism;
- fascism and race;
- the corporatist state;
- the concept of 'generic fascism'; and
- the specificity of National Socialism in Germany.

2 Core ideas of fascism

2.1 Anti-rationalism

The intellectual roots of fascism can be traced back to the voluntaristic idea that the *will* is prior to and superior to the *intellect* or reason. In most fascist ideologies, there is an emphasis on irrational concepts such as 'triumph of the will' and 'national destiny', which historians interpret as a *vitalist* revolt against reason. This world-view can be traced back to a range of intellectual sources, including writers as diverse as Friedrich Nietzsche (1844–1900), Georges Sorel (1847–1922) and Oswald Spengler (1880–1936).

The idea of a 'politics of the will' owes much to the philosopher Nietzsche, who challenged the prevailing view that human beings act in accordance with reason. For Nietzsche, it is not reason but the 'will to power' that drives human action — particularly the desire to dominate others. Nietzsche also believed that the masses require

leadership because they are only ever capable of rising to the level of a 'herd instinct'. Egalitarian concepts of democracy are nonsensical because they fail to acknowledge the existence of natural inequality. In place of democracy, he advocated a new elite of 'overlords' (*Übermenschen*) capable of providing the moral and intellectual leadership necessary for cultural progress. This idea of the overlord (or 'superman') was subsequently distorted by the Nazis into a theory of racial supremacy.

Another intellectual source of irrationalism was the French philosopher Georges Sorel, who believed that societies inevitably become decadent and disorganised as they reach a certain level of cultural development. Sorel detested liberal bourgeois society, and argued that decadence can be reversed only if the masses accept the absolute leadership of revolutionary idealists willing to use violence if necessary to achieve collective goals. He also argued that myth is a much more suitable device for mobilising the masses than class struggle, and believed that the revolutionary overthrow of bourgeois society could be brought about through the mythology of the general strike.

A similar idea was expressed by the conservative–revolutionary thinker Oswald Spengler, who argued in *The Decline of the West* that by celebrating commerce over culture and prudence over heroism, liberal capitalism has undermined the creative intellectual energies of Western civilisation. If the cultural foundations of European civilisation are further diluted and weakened, he suggested, this over-refined and decadent civilisation will inevitably collapse. From an elitist perspective, Spengler also believed that parliamentary democracy is self-destructive because it undermines the possibility of unified political leadership.

Note Anti-rationalists are essentially contemptuous of liberal democracy because it fails to provide the leadership necessary for achieving national unity.

This pessimistic, anti-democratic outlook was embraced by fascists in the 1920s and 1930s, but not in uniform ways. In France and Italy, fascist movements presented themselves as populist alternatives to socialism, while in Spain fascism was more influenced by *conservative elitism*. The negative consequences of anti-rationalism and anti-liberalism can be seen most clearly in German National Socialism.

2.2 Integral nationalism

Unlike classical nationalism, which asserts that the boundaries of the nation and the state should coincide, integral nationalism is based on the homogenisation of national identities, the expansion and racial improvement of the population, and a social Darwinist belief in the perpetual struggle of nations for survival. For this reason, fascist nationalism is opposed to liberal conceptions of citizenship where membership is based on democratic participation and civic patriotism.

Fascists glorify duty to the nation as the *highest political virtue*. In fascist ideologies the nation is understood in exclusive terms, and is both morally and politically superior to the individuals who comprise it. Using pseudo-biological metaphors, fascist ideologists stress the need for a regeneration of the organic 'race-nation', leading to the exclusion, forcible assimilation or even extermination of dissenting and minority groups.

Although the fascist concept of nationhood is based on *instinctive allegiance* rather than considered solidarity, fascism also draws on a national–populist tradition, which can be traced back to thinkers such as Rousseau, who criticised liberal concepts of democracy, emphasising instead a collectivist vision of the 'general will'. Rousseau maintained that modern states fail to create a sense of national unity because they do not articulate an *active concept of citizenship*. Although he believed in equality, Rousseau's critique of bourgeois civilisation and defence of popular sovereignty have influenced a variety of modern ideologies, including syndicalism and fascism.

For this reason, theorists of **totalitarianism** such as Jacob Talmon have drawn comparisons between the Jacobinism of the French revolutionaries and fascist **populism** in the 1920s. From an authoritarian–collectivist perspective, fascists argue that bourgeois society is too atomised and individualistic to provide an adequate focal point for mobilising the nation. This perception is reflected in the attempt to abolish all distinctions between private and public life and the demand for complete subservience to the state.

Note Some theorists have identified a Jacobin-style radicalism in fascist ideology. The Jacobins were left-wing bourgeois radicals who sought to create a nationally uniform and centralised government that truly expressed the sovereignty of the people.

However, the paradox of fascist nationalism is that it provides an unstable basis for political organisation. By creating unrealistic expectations of national glory and imperial expansion, fascism fails to establish a basis for the construction of durable political structures. Once fascist leaders embark on a project of expansion without reason, they are forced to divert resources away from reconstruction and regeneration towards destructive military campaigns.

This paradox is most clearly apparent in the barbaric and self-destructive Nazi plan to establish a 'Thousand-Year Reich' in Europe. Although Hitler offered to create a glorious future for the German people at the expense of the Slavs, Germany's defeat by the Soviet Union led to the break-up of the country in 1945. What had begun as opposition to the Versailles Treaty ended in a war of annihilation and genocide.

2.3 Authoritarian leadership

Fascists reject the liberal ideal of limited government based on constitutionalism and consent in favour of authoritarian leadership and a strong state. A basic assumption of fascist ideology is that strong leadership *simplifies* political decision-making, and that throughout history human societies have always been ruled — in one form or another — by dominant individuals. Abstract ideas such as democracy, egalitarianism and justice are thus caricatured as liberal 'fictions', which contradict the natural inequality of human beings and the need of the masses for strong leadership.

This critique of liberalism reflects a highly militaristic current in fascist thought. Fascist ideology is replete with references to martial virtues such as honour, virility, courage, duty, obedience and personal sacrifice. However, it is the figure of a charismatic leader which is most apparent in fascism: in all countries where fascism has been successful, unquestioning reverence of the leader and belief in the infallibility of the leader's vision, have been core features of the political system.

How can we explain this reverence for strong leadership, and why is it understood to be superior to parliamentary democracy? For Max Weber the answer lay in the personality of the charismatic ruler as a 'larger-than-life' figure. For Oswald Spengler, on the other hand, the answer lay in the distinction between the 'politician' and the 'statesman':

'The genuine statesman is distinguished from the 'mere politician'... by the fact that he dares to demand sacrifices — and obtains them, because his feeling that he is necessary to the time and the nation is shared by thousands, transforms them to the core, and renders them capable of deeds to which otherwise they could never have risen.'

It is this vision of inspirational leadership that finds its clearest expression in historical figures such as Adolf Hitler and Benito Mussolini. In Germany, Hitler was portrayed as the Führer, or ultimate leader, while Mussolini was referred to as Il Duce. Other leaders of fascist movements have adopted titles such as Conducator, or Generalissimo, suggesting a level of infallibility, resoluteness and strength unavailable to democratic politicians.

2.4 Corporatism

As well as stressing leadership, fascist ideologies emphasise a traditional conservative conception of society as a 'harmonious organic social order'. **Corporatism**, in its original form, was a social system based on the organisation of society into a system of 'estates' and 'corporations'. This idea has its roots in the medieval guilds, which functioned as *intermediate structures* between rulers and subjects, regulating everyday interaction and promoting civic cohesion.

Romantic anti-capitalists see corporatism as a means for *recreating social harmony and economic stability*. Their goal is to reduce alienation and **anomy** in modern civilisation: because capitalist societies are atomised and fragmented, lacking cohesion, it is essential to promote integration by reinvigorating a sense of community and common endeavour. However, it is only in fascism that corporatism emerged as a populist 'third way' between capitalism and socialism, offering fascist rulers an alternative to parliamentary democracy and autonomous interest representation as vehicles for political and economic integration.

Fascist corporatism has assumed two main forms:
- *State corporatism*. In Italy, the Fascist state sought to promote cooperation between employers and workers in the interests of achieving national economic objectives. The aim was to regulate the market economy without introducing social ownership or state planning, by forcing employers to join state-administered cartels, and obliging workers to join state-administered trade unions. In one sense, this meant recognising the *de facto* emergence of cartels as a feature of monopolistic capitalism, but as a form of economic regulation it also increased the power of the state over the economy.

Note Fascist corporatism in Italy forced both employers and workers to cooperate in the realisation of national economic goals, increasing the power of the state over the economy.

- *The racial state*. In Nazi Germany a very different form of corporatism emerged, based on the concept of the *Volksgemeinschaft* (people's racial community). This model of political organisation drew on romantic anti-capitalist traditions, seeking to replace a 'degenerate' cosmopolitan society with a culturally homogeneous national community. It also sought to establish *racial identity* as the core legitimating principle in the fascist state, making membership contingent on ethnicity and identity rather than on patriotism or civic pride.

Fascist corporatism appeals to marginalised groups (*déclassés*) threatened by rapid social and economic change. This was most obviously the case among the *Mittelstand* (lower middle class) in Weimar Germany, who were negatively affected by economic crisis and political instability. However, while these groups did provide electoral support for fascist movements such as the Nazis, in practice middle-class radicalism fails to reduce the political and economic power of large employers and organised labour in the modern industrial state.

Ultimately, fascist corporatism can be seen as a form of *managed capitalism*, which seeks to reconcile private ownership with the pursuit of collectivist goals — chiefly by mobilising the working class behind the nationalist goals of the regime. This strategy is also evident in national–populist ideologies such as Perónism in Argentina in the 1940s and 1950s, where it was used to integrate the newly urbanised masses behind an authoritarian elite without altering property relations.

One of the key differences between populism and fascism is the extent to which labour organisations are accorded influence in the regime. Emerging during a period of rapid modernisation, Perónism unified a variety of groups, from military leaders to socialists, who all found something to support in Perón's patriotic programme — including labour leaders who were allowed a degree of political influence and control over their organisations. Under fascism, by contrast, autonomous labour organisations were abolished and socialist leaders arrested or killed, leading to a *fusion of corporate and state power*. Unfortunately, in Argentina, General Perón fatally weakened the labour movement, and his eventual defeat paved the way for a brutal military dictatorship (1976–82), which some commentators compare to fascism in its use of state-sanctioned violence.

Note There are similarities between fascism and populism, chiefly in their capacity to unify a wide range of groups behind the agenda of powerful elites.

2.5 Racialism

Not all fascist ideologies are explicitly racialist, but most fascists adopt a **chauvinistic** or jingoistic attitude towards rival national groups, based either on racialist or culturalist assumptions. Unlike Nazism, Italian fascism was primarily concerned with political goals, and did not introduce **anti-Semitic** race laws until 1938. However, Italians regarded Africans as an 'inferior race', which helped to justify Mussolini's expansionist policy in Libya and Abyssinia.

Racialists believe that the genetic character of different human racial sub-groups has important political and cultural consequences. Racialism was a feature of the 'civilising mission ideology' of the European colonial powers, and theories of racial supremacy and racial conflict were developed by thinkers such as Arthur de Gobineau (1816–82) and Houston Stewart Chamberlain (1855–1939). Chamberlain was an English intellectual who embraced German culture. Like many contemporaries, he believed in the superior character of the 'Nordic' race — that is, the Celtic and Germanic peoples of Northern and Western Europe. At the root of this ideology is the belief that the Nordic people constitute a 'racial elite' at the apex of the hierarchy of human racial sub-groups. To retain this elite status, the Nordic people must preserve and defend their racial inheritance against dilution from 'inferior', i.e. non-European, groups. The ideological justification for this belief is the assumption that all civilisations must be judged by their cultural and technical achievements. For white supremacists, the superiority of the Nordic people is supposedly based on the sophistication of European civilisation in comparison with the 'less advanced' culture of non-Europeans.

This racial mythology was a convenient resource in nineteenth-century European imperialism. Although they expressed it in less explicit terms, European colonists justified their territorial acquisition and exploitation as an unfortunate but necessary consequence of the attempt to 'civilise' the non-white races of the world, leading to the popular myth of the 'white man's burden' and the necessity of empire. Elements of this myth persist in a more subtle form today in the 'liberal imperialism' of American neoconservatism.

In some forms of fascism, there is an explicit attempt to justify the racial superiority of the European peoples against the 'racial contamination' of non-European peoples. This was expressed most forcefully in the anti-Semitic ideology of National Socialism, which linked the future of the 'Aryan' people to the destruction of the Jewish race and the colonisation of territory in Eastern Europe. However, in their attempt to 'purify' the German nation, the Nazis not only exterminated the European Jews, but also attempted to eliminate homosexuals, the mentally ill, the disabled, and other groups considered 'unworthy of human life'. Fascist racialism can also be seen in the following examples:

- The racial mythology of Romanian fascism, based on a romanticised concept of the Dacian people as descendants of the Italo–Germanic tribes of central Europe. The Iron Guard regime allied itself with the Nazis and cooperated in the transportation of an estimated 850,000 Jews from the territory of Greater Romania to extermination camps in Poland.
- The Lebanese Phalangist movement, which defended the 'unique' culture of the Maronite Christian community of the Levant against the encroachment of Pan-Arabist and Islamic ideologies. The Phalange were responsible for the massacre of thousands of Palestinian refugees in the Israeli invasion of Lebanon in 1982.
- The 'clerical fascism' of the Croatian Ustaše. During the early 1940s, this movement of Catholic extremists tried to destroy the Serbian Orthodox community in Croatia through systematic genocide, expulsion and religious conversion, in an attempt to create an ethnically pure Croatian nation. The savage violence of the Ustaše shocked even the Nazi occupation forces in Serbia, and led to bitter reprisals after the war.

Note The Ustaše were wiped out in post-war Yugoslavia, but Croatian nationalists finally succeeded in establishing an independent state in 1992.

3 Theories of fascism

Fascism and traditional authoritarianism often appear superficially similar, but there are important distinctions between these ideological traditions. We can differentiate fascism from authoritarianism by comparing the following features:

Fascism	Traditional authoritarianism
Right-wing/expansionist	Right-wing/militarist
Charismatic leader principle	Oligarchical leadership, e.g. military junta
Mass activist politics/politicisation of everyday life	Suppression of politics
Populist	Elitist
Corporatist economic policies	Defence of existing economic interests
Mass terror/coercion/organised violence	Human rights abuses/torture
Anti-clerical	Support for organised religion

Fascism asserts the need for order, authority, hierarchy and discipline, but — unlike authoritarianism — undermines the possibility of sustaining durable political structures. The tendency is captured well by the Spanish conservative writer, José Ortega y Gasset (1883–1955), who observed that:

'Fascism has an enigmatic countenance because in it appear the most counterposed contents. It asserts authoritarianism and organises rebellion. It fights against contemporary democracy and, on the other hand, does not believe in the restoration of any past rule. It seems to forge itself as the forge of a strong state, and uses means most conducive to its dissolution, as if it were a destructive faction of a secret society.'

As the Italian historian Emilio Gentile argues, the key to understanding fascism is to differentiate between its 'movement phase' and its 'regime phase'.

- During the movement phase, fascist parties emerge *outside* the framework of parliamentary politics, and participate in elections only to gain credibility and publicity. At this stage, there is often little to distinguish between fascism and other syndicalist movements opposed to the liberal–capitalist system.
- In the regime phase, however, fascists enter into tactical alliances with existing elites who view the movement as a means to reorganise their social base and increase their own political power during periods of rapid economic change and social crisis. Unlike traditional authoritarianism, which is based on oligarchical leadership and the suppression of politics, fascism appeals to middle-class and working-class voters by appearing to offer a populist alternative to capitalism and socialism.

Nevertheless, there is much disagreement between historians and social scientists over the causes and nature of fascism. This disagreement centres on the uniqueness of historical fascism in the inter-war period, and the possibility of defining a generic type of fascist ideology based on a single key component.

3.1 The liberal–historical school

Liberal historians typically portray fascism as a unique political phenomenon, fuelled by the growth of irrational and mythical ideas. By advocating the organising power myth over reason, fascism draws on powerful anti-rationalist currents in European culture and society in a 'revolt against reason'. As Professor Noël O'Sullivan argues, the rise of fascism in the 1920s reflected the growing sense of disillusionment in Europe after 1918 with the 'limited' style of politics inherited from the nineteenth century, and the desire for more radical and direct forms of political engagement.

Acccording to the politician and writer Benedetto Croce (1866–1952), therefore, the transition to fascism in the 1920s was not the result of structural crisis, but of a 'collapse of conscience, a civil depression and [an] intoxication produced by the First World War'. This enabled extreme nationalists to rally support against the perceived injustice of the Versailles Treaty of 1919, which left large numbers of Europeans under foreign rule. In this sense, liberals see fascism as a deviation from the 'normal' path of history. It is not a 'generic' feature of European civilisation, but a unique phenomenon that was successful where:

- liberal–democratic traditions were less established;
- nationalist aspirations were unsatisfied;

- political polarisation was more extreme; and
- existing forms of representation lacked legitimacy.

The principal countries where fascism was successful were Italy and Germany, which were both 'belated nations' (nation-states created late by European standards), and lacked a cohesive national bourgeoisie. According to the liberal–historical school, the ruling elite in Germany and Italy failed to embrace parliamentarism, and instead projected a nationalist agenda aimed at restoring a 'glorious past'. The weakness of this view is clear in two main ways:

- During the inter-war years, fascist movements and parties appeared in more than a dozen countries in Europe and elsewhere (including France and Britain) where national-unity governments helped to stabilise the political situation. In no countries did fascism come to power without the support of local elites.
- Fascism is less a deviation from the 'normal' course of modern European history than a political feature of societies undergoing rapid economic change and social disloca-tion. Right-wing populist movements are a consistent feature of modernising societies, and fascism cannot be explained purely by its appeal to anti-rationalist myth.

While fascism in its historical form is clearly unrepeatable, the conditions that facili-tate fascism are not. The union of economic and political power, the growth of milita-rism and the rise of right-wing populism can conspire to undermine democracy in a range of political situations.

3.2 The Marxist theory of fascism

During the late nineteenth century, politics was dominated by established liberal and conservative elites committed to the defence of industry and empire. According to Marxist theory, the key problem of politics lay in the need to integrate the working class into the mainstream political community. In Germany, France, Italy and Britain, this was partially achieved by means of three political–ideological strategies:

- national–imperialism (colonial adventures provided an ideal diversion from the problems of class conflict on the domestic front);
- 'political transformism', aimed at neutralising the contradiction between the ruling-power elite and the masses by means of petty-bourgeois popular-democratic parties; and
- reformism and trade unionism as methods for mitigating the negative impact of the market.

Note For Marxists the rise of fascism is closely linked to the crisis tendencies in the capitalist system at a certain stage of economic development.

Like liberal historians, Marxists see the First World War as a defining moment in the crisis of industrial class society. By undermining the international economic system and plunging the nations of Europe into a murderous conflict, the war ushered in a new era of inter-imperialist rivalry and economic nationalism. Most importantly, however, the profitability of the capitalist system was undermined, and with it the pre-war system of political–ideological stabilisation. From a Marxist perspective, therefore, a process of crisis was set in motion. *The paradox of fascism is that the state is forced to resort to a strategy of repression and mass mobilisation in order to stabilise society.* Ernesto Laclau, author of *Politics and Ideology in Marxist Theory*, summarises this perspective as follows:

- Industrial society enters a period of crisis during the transition from *competitive* to *monopoly* capitalism; capitalism becomes increasingly unstable as a result of internal contradictions, which increase the necessity for state intervention in the economy and society.
- Unable to stabilise the crisis through the existing power structure, monopoly capitalism is forced to confront the political apparatus of the state by basing itself on a new radical mass movement 'disconnected' from any authentic socialist worldview.
- The assault on parliamentary democracy results in the assumption of power by the fascist party, which then eliminates its more radical collectivist elements.
- An exceptional form of dictatorship is created to defend capitalist interests, which abolishes pluralism and attempts to integrate workers through a campaign of mass mobilisation and national aggrandisement.

This process is exemplified by the use of mass mobilisation in Germany in the 1930s as the country engaged in reconstruction. The Nazi state marshalled all the resources of state and society for rearmament, causing structural imbalances in the economy. Yet the economic policies of the Nazi regime greatly benefited industrialists, who were able to increase production without reducing prices, and who were able to take advantage of a politically weakened labour force.

3.3 Fascism as totalitarianism

Note The concept of totalitarianism was popular among Cold War liberals in the 1950s. It was convenient to categorise fascism and communism as varieties of totalitarianism, on the basis that both are anti-pluralist.

An alternative approach focuses on the idea that fascism is simply another form of totalitarianism. This view implies that fascism — like Stalinism — is based on the idea of a 'total state', where the state demands the complete subordination of the individual in the interests of national unity, and where the state attempts to impose total control over an atomised society. According to Hannah Arendt, author of *The Origins of Totalitarianism*, totalitarianism may be seen as a response to four historical processes:

- the decline of the traditional nation-state;
- the decline of authority;
- the atomisation of mass society; and
- the crisis of the class system.

Totalitarianism represents an attempt to address these structural problems through the complete subordination of individuals to the collective, through the projection of national unity, and through social regimentation.

The first country that experimented with this type of political system was Italy under Mussolini, who recognised the weakness of traditional bourgeois politics as a means for unifying the Italian people. The fascist regime in Italy sought to end the distinction between the public and private spheres, and attempted to integrate the capitalist economy within a corporatist structure designed to overcome class divisions and impose discipline and order.

There is clearly a link between fascism and totalitarianism, as both systems display the following features:

- emphasis on the 'total state';
- supreme-leader principle (charismatic leader);
- politicisation of everyday life;
- severe erosion of civil liberties;
- terror and state-sanctioned violence;
- ideological indoctrination; and
- expansionist foreign policy.

Some political theorists have also tried to depict Soviet communism as a type of totalitarianism. There are indeed many similarities — both systems emphasising collectivism and employing terror and mass indoctrination — but the economic system of the Soviet Union was characterised by state ownership of the means of production, whereas in Germany and Italy private capitalism was allowed to continue.

One of the weaknesses of totalitarianism theory is that it overlooks the different emphasis on collectivisation in Stalinism. Unlike fascist regimes, the Soviet Union abolished private ownership, replacing the market with a state-planned economy. Totalitarianism is also more an *aspiration* than a reality. Even in Nazi Germany the state failed to achieve absolute control over the individual, and the short lifespan of fascist regimes suggests that they are ultimately unstable and fundamentally unsuited to the organisational complexity of modern industrial societies.

3.4 Revisionist approaches

Using a comparative–analytic approach, revisionist historians focus on what is common between fascist, neofascist and national–populist ideologies, rather than the structural or economic nature of fascist regimes. Implicit in their work is an emphasis on cultural rather than political factors. Historians such as Roger Griffin and Stanley Payne argue that earlier theories of generic fascism are not very useful. They suggest that, while fascist movements and regimes differ in important ways, Nazism, Italian Fascism, Falangism and other lesser examples of fascism belong to the same essential family of nationalist ideologies.

For Griffin, fascism (at least in its early movement phase) is not a *reactionary* political force but a *revolutionary* nationalist movement. The generic basic feature of fascism is *palingenetic* nationalism, a specific type of modernist nationalism devoted to the rebirth and regeneration of the nation-state. Although Griffin has been accused of *essentialism* (reducing a complex phenomenon to one of its key variables), his theory of generic fascism has been highly influential.

Payne's typology of fascist ideologies offers a more comprehensive method for evaluating the phenomenon. Payne argues that we must examine the goals of fascism and the organisational forms of fascist politics, as well as the things fascism *negates*. His typology can be summarised as follows:

Ideology and goals:
- Vitalist philosophy
- Nationalist authoritarian state
- Integrated national economy (corporatism)
- Imperialism/expansionary nationalism

Fascist negations:
- Anti-liberalism
- Anti-socialism
- Anti-rationalism

Style and organisation:
- Mass mobilisation/militarisation
- Aesthetic visual appeal (mass meetings and symbols, rituals, politics as religion)
- Emphasis on masculinity and virility/patriarchy
- Youth over age (appeal to the next generation)

3.5 Evaluation

Each of these theories offers a different perspective on fascism, and valid insights. There is, however, a gulf between approaches that see fascism as a *revolutionary* mass movement, and those that see it as a *reactionary* force committed to the defence of established interests.

Broadly speaking, liberals and Marxists agree that fascism is a reactionary ideology opposed to Enlightenment rationalism, but disagree about the social basis of fascist movements. For liberals, fascism is a quintessentially *extra-parliamentary* force, defined in its opposition to established liberal and conservative institutions, which attracts support from younger workers. For Marxists, fascism begins as a radical mass movement from the streets, but acquires respectability in an attempt to appeal to middle-class voters, before being co-opted and mobilised by conservative elites in defence of anti-democratic goals. Marxists point to Italy, Spain and Germany as examples of this process.

Against this view, totalitarianism theorists emphasise the distinction between fascism and earlier forms of right-wing radicalism. They argue that fascism has its roots in the mass tendencies of modern society in which traditional forms of authority and identity are undermined. Fascism is 'modern' in the sense that it adopts new and radical forms of social and political organisation, but is reactionary in the sense that it leads to a new type of political barbarism.

Against all of these views, revisionist theories of generic fascism emphasise the authentic revolutionary identity of fascism as a modernist and nationalist movement committed to the regeneration of a decadent liberal society. They insist that we must 'take fascism seriously', even though fascist ideology lacks any coherent theoretical basis.

In the final analysis, revisionist theories that posit fascism as an 'ideal type' (a revolutionary nationalist ideology with similar features irrespective of historical and cultural conditions) fail to account for the links between fascism and capitalism, and the links between fascism and imperialism. Fascist movements appear to offer an alternative to the existing framework of capitalism, but despite some novel interventions in the market there is no attempt to alter property relations and no 'cultural revolution' under fascism in its regime phase. Furthermore, revisionists fail to account for the very real differences between examples of fascism, particularly the distinction between fascism in Germany and Eastern Europe, and fascism in Mediterranean countries. These differences can be seen in the table below, which highlights the major similarities and differences between fascist movements:

Nation	Movement	Leader	Ideology
UK	British Union of Fascists	Oswald Mosley	Social imperialism, corporatism, Unionism
Croatia	Ustaše	Anton Pavelić	Racialism, expansionist nationalism, clericalism
France	Le Faisceau	Georges Valois	Integral nationalism, corporatism, syndicalism
Germany	NSDAP	Adolf Hitler	Racial imperialism, anti-Semitism, imperialism
Hungary	Arrow Cross	Ferenc Szálasi	Racialism, anti-Semitism, expansionist nationalism
Italy	Fascist Party of Italy	Benito Mussolini	Imperialism, integral nationalism, corporatism
Portugal	Estado Novo	Antonio Salazar	Integral nationalism, authoritarianism, clericalism
Spain	Falange Española	José Antonio Primo de Rivera	Integral nationalism, clericalism, conservatism
Romania	League of Archangel Michael	Cornelieu Codreanu	Racialism, anti-Semitism, mystical nationalism

4 The specificity of National Socialism

In contrast to economic corporatism in Italy, where the state presided over a tripartite alliance with capital and labour, corporatism in Nazi Germany was understood in explicitly racialist terms as an attempt to create an ethnically pure Aryan state. As with Italian fascism, there was an emphasis on the failure of traditional liberal politics to integrate the different social classes of modern industrial society.

In Germany, however, 'society' itself was redefined by ideologists as an exclusive ethnic concept: national unity was possible only through the elimination of 'harmful alien' influences. In an attempt to recast the *Volk* (people) as an exclusive unit, Nazi ideologists differentiated between the traditional ideal of a community based on affective ties (*Gemeinschaft*) and the modern idea of a society as an association of individuals (*Gesellschaft*).

The traditional *Gemeinschaft* was seen to embody the virtues of order, duty, uniformity and integration. Nazi propaganda focused on the idea of 'blood and soil' as the defining features of nationhood, using imagery of sturdy German peasants labouring uncritically and unselfconsciously for the good of the community. The Nazis idealised the small-town community as the authentic German way of life, where traditional structures and values, e.g. patriarchy, obedience, duty and family honour are preserved.

This image was contrasted with the modern cosmopolitan idea of society as an association of individuals bound together by much looser ties than exist in traditional communities. In the modern *Gesellschaft*, the lives of individuals are less regulated and integration is weaker, encouraging individualism, nonconformism and cultural diversity. The symbol of the modern *Gesellschaft* was 1920s Berlin, a metropolis characterised by its 'rootless cosmopolitanism', mixed population, cultural decadence, crime and disorder.

Understood from this perspective, the principal message of Nazi propaganda was *anti-modern*: rural and provincial culture was good, the metropolis was bad. Although this made little sense in real terms (Germany was and remained a modern industrial class society), the Nazis used such propaganda as a technique for mobilising support against supposedly harmful social influences.

The primary aim of National Socialism was to purify the German nation of 'harmful influences' by promoting not simply a common culture (the typical strategy of nationalists) but a *homogeneous racial identity*.

Whereas traditional anti-Semitism was based on fear and prejudice towards Jewish people, Nazi anti-Semitism was strongly influenced by **eugenics**, a pseudo-scientific doctrine holding that social and cultural problems such as mental illness or criminality are genetically inherited. Supporters of the eugenics movement believed that negative human traits could be eliminated by identifying the source of the trait in 'deviant' families and by using sterilisation to prevent individuals from reproducing.

Note Eugenics was also popular in the USA at this time. Eugenicists advocated sterilisation of criminals and the promotion of a healthy, racially homogeneous 'middle-class' society.

In its simplest form, Nazi racial theory portrayed the Jewish people as racial *bacilli* 'infecting' an otherwise healthy Aryan nation. Along with the Sinti and Roma (Gypsies), Jews were placed at the bottom of the racial hierarchy, and caricatured as parasitic aliens. Only by eliminating this alien influence could the German people defend their racial purity, an idea which ultimately led to the extermination camps of Auschwitz, Bełzec, Maidanek and Treblinka. This racialist ideology was shared, albeit in less extreme forms, by other right-wing nationalists and fascists in Eastern Europe, who actively participated in the Final Solution and the war against the USSR.

However, Nazi ideology linked the Jewish presence to two contradictory influences, namely finance capitalism and communism. Playing on German fears of economic ruin and political instability, the Nazis portrayed the Jews as the masters of a worldwide anti-German conspiracy, manipulating the banks in Wall Street and the Bolsheviks in Russia. Although it is absurd to suggest that such an alliance could exist, it was a successful propaganda tool, given the disproportionate number of Jews in banking and finance and the large number of Bolsheviks who also happened to be Jews.

At the other extreme, Nazi racial ideology celebrated the unique and superior virtues of the 'Aryan master race', which occupied the highest place in the racial hierarchy. Members of the SS had to be able to demonstrate their pure German ancestry dating back to the eighteenth century, in order to prevent racial 'contamination'. The SS became a feared racial elite, with its own schools, police and 'breeding' policy. Even within the short timespan of the Third Reich (1933–45) it created a system of racial persecution and mass extermination that has become synonymous with evil.

The cynical processing of human beings in the interests of racial purity resulted in genocide and the brutal exploitation of millions of prisoners of war in labour camps. More than any other event, the Holocaust underlines the irrational dimension of nationalism and racialism, but many other cases of genocide have occurred since 1945, for example in Yugoslavia, Rwanda and, more recently, Sudan.

5 Neofascism and the far right

Despite the horrors of the Second World War and the Holocaust, right-wing extremists in Europe and North America continue to believe that fascism offers a viable alternative to the liberal–democratic, pluralist framework of modern society. For a variety of reasons, including fear, economic uncertainty, chauvinism and racialism, nationalists, neofascists and white supremacists continue to politicise ethnicity, advocating a policy of defensive integration based on the white, monoglot community.

After 1945, neofascism was a marginal political force in Europe, restricted to the fringes of politics. Many former fascists and ex-Nazis melted into the new political structures growing up in Eastern and Western Europe, and political radicalisation was held in check by the ideological and military stand-off between NATO and the Warsaw Pact. Yet a resurgence of right-wing activism took place in the 1970s, partly as a backlash against the New Left, and partly as a reaction against non-white immigration.

This is epitomised by the support for Enoch Powell among sections of the English working class, and the rise of the National Front (NF) under John Tyndall. The NF preached a white supremacism and **xenophobic** nationalism, and warned of the dangers of multiculturalism and racial mixing, but the movement failed to take off in electoral terms and went into decline in the 1980s.

The resurgence of right-wing extremism in Europe came after the collapse of state socialism in Eastern Europe and the move towards closer European political and economic integration in Western Europe in the 1990s. These changes have increased support for parties of the right who oppose established parliamentary politics and offer populist solutions to the problems of post-industrial societies. The advance of the far right also highlights the erosion of alternatives to liberal capitalism and popular anxiety about globalisation. With the collapse of socialism, disillusioned voters now seek populist alternatives to the mainstream parties of the centre-left and centre-right, and, as Pippa Norris (author of *Radical Right: Parties and Electoral Competition*) argues, the radical right has adapted its policies and image to suit this new political landscape.

Note The resurgence of the far right since the 1990s reflects growing anxieties over globalisation. Many voters seek refuge in far-right parties that claim to offer a set of simpler alternatives based on ethnicity and identity.

The advance of the far right can be seen most clearly in Austria, France and Italy, where right-wing populists have advanced in the electoral marketplace by responding to xenophobic public opinion:

- In Austria, the two far-right parties currently hold between them 29% of the seats in the national parliament.
- In Italy, Silvio Berlusconi's ruling right-wing populist coalition is comprised of parties such as the Northern League and Alleanza Nazionale, both of which are identified with neofascism.
- In France, Jean-Marie Le Pen's National Front came second in the first round of the 2002 presidential election, before being defeated by Jacques Chirac in the second round.

In the UK, the growth of the far right has been less dramatic, although the British National Party (BNP) has acquired greater credibility and respectability by shedding its racist image and competing on an anti-establishment platform. This policy has yielded mixed results for, although the BNP gained two seats in the European Parliament at

the June 2009 elections, it is still seen by most voters as an extremist party (or 'party of protest') rather than a serious contender for political office.

A key question remains: whether the resurgence of the far right since the 1990s can be compared with the rise of fascism in the 1920s. Roger Eatwell, author of *Fascism: A History*, warns against drawing simplistic parallels between historical fascism and the modern far right. He argues that, while right-wing extremists still connect fascist themes such as identity and race, and the far right is still associated with violence and paramilitarism, modern-day far-right parties actually represent a more isolated constituency than inter-war fascists. From a sociological perspective, typical neofascist supporters conform to the following profile:

- white male;
- working class/lower middle class;
- socially marginalised;
- unemployed/uneducated/unskilled; and
- lacking experience of a multicultural environment.

There is an element of revivalism in right-wing populism that is opposed to the 'disenchanted pragmatism' of modern politics. The principal effect of the resurgence of the far right in Europe has been to create a populist backlash against immigration and multiculturalism. This strategy appeals mainly, but not exclusively, to disaffected voters who feel that mainstream parties no longer authentically represent their views, and that the liberal political establishment has become detached from ordinary voters.

Key terms and concepts

Anomy	A condition of social instability resulting from a breakdown of values or from a lack of moral purpose or ideals
Anti-Semitism	Hatred and suspicion of Jews
Chauvinism	Contempt for foreigners, based on the assumption of national superiority
Corporatism	The theory and practice of organising economy and society into corporations subordinate to the state
Eugenics	A pseudo-science dedicated to the elimination of 'genetically transmitted' social ills, e.g. criminality, insanity
Integral nationalism	A type of nationalism that stresses the homogenisation and improvement of the 'race-nation'
Populism	A style of politics where rulers emphasise an abstract feature of society that seems to underlie all social grievances, usually diverting attention from real political issues
Romantic anti-capitalism	Yearning for the simplicity of a pre-industrial past, particularly those cultural features of traditional communities that are lost in the process of capitalist modernisation
Totalitarianism	An authoritarian system of government based on the 'total state' and the politicisation of everyday life
Vitalism	A naturalist philosophical world-view emphasising the importance of life-force and will rather than reason or intellect
Xenophobia	Dislike or fear of foreigners

CHAPTER 7 Feminism

1 Introduction

Students who study feminism must ensure they do not view the topic as an easy option and succumb to oversimplification or generalisation. Feminism is a complex ideological world-view, which intersects in important ways with liberalism, socialism, ecologism and multiculturalism. Those who are aware of these links will be able to differentiate clearly between the different schools (or waves) of feminist theory, their relevance for mainstream political ideologies, and their relative success in challenging women's oppression.

Feminism recasts the traditional language of politics by shifting the emphasis of debate toward *relations between the sexes*. Feminists maintain that women are disadvantaged and discriminated against because of **sex** and **gender** differences, and that male domination is perpetuated in society through the ideological reproduction of patriarchal values and relations, and by excluding sexual politics from the normal channels of political debate.

Feminism is not a single monolithic ideology but a set of political and ideological responses to sexual inequality and male domination. The earliest feminist thinkers adopted a liberal humanist approach, believing that women should not be targets of legal subjugation or political discrimination on the grounds of sexual difference. Humanists reject the idea that women should be treated differently, arguing that men and women share a common human nature and should be treated equally.

However, 'second-wave' feminists reject this view, and stress instead a *gynocentric* approach, believing that men and women are sufficiently different to warrant a more exclusive focus on feminine moral psychology and specifically feminine issues. Both of these views are rejected by Marxist feminists, who reiterate the primacy of class in sociological debates, and by postmodern feminists who reject universalising narratives of gender and identity in favour of localising approaches to sexual inequality and oppression.

Key issues and debates
- the separation of the personal and political;
- the feminist critique of patriarchy;
- the social construction of gender;
- differences between liberal and radical feminism;
- overlaps and tensions between feminism and Marxism;
- the absence of conservative feminism;
- the postmodern turn in feminism; and
- post-feminism.

2 Core ideas of feminism

2.1 The personal and the political

Feminists argue that mainstream politics and political theory either ignore or downplay the impact of the personal sphere on the public sphere. In feminist political theory, by contrast, there is an explicit link between the private sphere and the public sphere. Feminists maintain that the division of labour in society is determined by the division of labour within the family, that relations between the sexes within the family *structure* the relations of domination and subordination in society as a whole.

Even the division between the personal and political is gendered. The public sphere is seen as a traditionally 'male' preserve, while the private sphere is a 'female' preserve, the one area of human social activity over which women traditionally exert control. This separation perpetuates an anachronistic view of women's place in the world, which — even in Western countries — prevents women from achieving equality with men.

Although there are important differences in the way liberal and radical feminists see the personal/political divide (see below), most agree that the definition of what constitutes 'the political' should be extended to cover the politics of gender and the politics of sexual equality. Radical feminist thinkers such as Kate Millett argue that the identification of the private sphere with the feminine is so deeply ingrained in our civilisation that it has developed a kind of 'natural', taken-for-granted status. For this reason, 'women's issues' are always relegated to the margins of the political, just as 'women's history' in academia is still often relegated to the fringes of mainstream scholarship.

Note Feminists complain that many of the issues that matter most to women are simply not discussed by mainstream political parties.

The notion that women should assume a subservient role as homemakers and mothers has a hegemonic quality that is difficult to challenge. Although women possess *formal* equality (in law), many men and women continue to believe it is right and proper that women should assume a nurturing role in view of their biological characteristics. Conversely, because men are said to be more 'rational' and 'emotionally stronger', so it is right that they should be engaged in serious worldly activities such as politics, business and science.

This socially constructed prejudice is often combined with a vague form of **biological determinism**, based on the view that women are designed for child-rearing and should thus aspire to (and be content with) this role rather than compete with men for occupational status. Despite the increasing presence of women in the workforce, the notion that women should occupy traditionally 'masculine' positions of authority is still widely rejected.

2.2 Anti-patriarchy

At the heart of feminist analysis is the concept of **patriarchy**, which refers to the domination of men over women in society. Historically, a 'patriarchy' is a family, state or society controlled by dominant men, especially senior patriarchs (male heads of extended families). The term 'patriarchy' was, as we shall see in more detail below, introduced by radical gynocentric feminists to distinguish between those social forces which reproduce sexism and female subjugation from other social forces (such as capitalist relations of production) which reproduce class inequalities.

Note For radical feminists the origins of female inequality lie in the institutionalisation of patriarchy.

Patriarchy is not simply an idea or belief held by sexist men, but a social relation that varies between societies, depending on the extent of male domination within different spheres of social, economic and cultural activity. It is the continuous reproduction of this social relation over time that perpetuates inequality and segregation between the sexes. These are transformed into socio–cultural patterns, which are in turn experienced and assimilated as normal and everyday by new generations. For feminists, the operation of patriarchy can be seen in a variety of settings:

- In economic terms, male control of the labour market is viewed as the main cause of gender inequality and segregation. Because men control most positions of authority and command in society (vertical segregation), there is a tendency to equate seniority with gender. Although some women may be equally qualified to perform key leadership roles, they are excluded because female candidates are considered unsuitable for senior roles.
- In socio–cultural terms, male control of the media is seen as responsible for the reproduction of traditional relations of domination. Through the monopolisation of senior executive jobs, and through the depiction of men and women in familiar dominant and submissive roles, the media continually reaffirm the patriarchal relations that govern society.

Feminists argue that the institutionalisation of patriarchy can be seen in the way that science embodies the domination of male values and perspectives, which is exacerbated by the dominant position of men in academia. Feminists use the term *malestream* to distinguish the values and perspectives that govern mainstream science. They argue that the malestream standpoint is rooted in the institution of patriarchy, and that the technical, objective, rational character of scientific knowledge privileges a 'male' way of looking at the world in which the emphasis is on 'hard' facts and the compartmentalisation of knowledge into ever smaller categories of things with similar characteristics.

2.3 The social construction of gender

Alongside the reproduction of patriarchy, feminists reject deterministic arguments that legitimise the subservient role of women as wives and mothers by emphasising inherited biological characteristics. Anti-feminists argue that men are physically stronger and more aggressive and thus more suited to strenuous manual labour and 'tough' managerial roles, while women are weaker and more gentle and thus more suited to caring, nurturing roles. This cliched view of male and female capabilities is reproduced at the level of everyday social interaction and exchange, and such ingrained prejudices are difficult to challenge rationally.

In the broadest sense, argues feminist theorist Professor Sally Haslanger, something is 'socially constructed' if it is an 'intended or unintended product of a social practice'. From this perspective, feminists reject the thesis of biological determinism, according to which biology determines destiny, arguing that what most people see as 'essential' biological facts about men and women are in fact socially and culturally reproduced.

To understand the feminist critique, therefore, it is essential to differentiate clearly between the terms 'sex' and 'gender':
- 'Sex' refers to the inherited biological features that differentiate men and women. The male/female distinction stems from differences in relation to reproductive activity: women are equipped for child-bearing, while men perform only a marginal role.
- 'Gender' refers to the received social and cultural assumptions about sexual difference. From a feminist perspective, gender is a purely random or artificial construction (although patterns are clearly identifiable). Gender roles are learned rather than inherited, and the facts of biology should not be used to dictate a woman's fate in society.

Anti-feminists insist that the child-bearing role of women conditions them for a child-rearing role. From a feminist perspective, however, sexual identity is more than simply a biological fact, and feminists reject the arguments of evolutionary psychology that genetic inheritance conditions social and cultural development. Sexual identity is a biological fact with important social implications: men and women represent distinct social groups, but the character of these groups has nothing to do with masculine or feminine 'nature'.

Feminist sociologists stress this point strongly. They argue that 'gender' is what happens when cultures reformulate what begins as a fact of nature: through socialisation and the assimilation of cultural norms, the sexes are redefined, represented and channelled into different roles in culturally specific ways. Just as new immigrants assimilate into their new host culture through adaptation and socialisation, so women acquire the social and cultural traits that mark them out as women in given contexts. In French feminist Simone de Beauvoir's famous remark, one is not 'born' but 'becomes' a woman by identifying with and acquiring predetermined gender traits.

Feminists thus draw a distinction between biologically and culturally determined behaviour in order to emancipate both women and men from narrowly defined gender roles. While there are important differences between liberal and radical feminists regarding the determining role of nature, the emphasis is on understanding the distinctiveness of male and female groups without imposing identity and without making female distinctiveness a cause for discrimination.

Note Consider how much less rigid the gender divide has become in Western societies. It is now permissible for men and women to adopt dress codes that would once have been considered 'deviant'.

2.4 Gender equality

Early feminists were concerned with the issue of political equality, specifically the achievement of a universal franchise. In Britain, full political equality was achieved in 1928, and for early advocates of women's rights this represented a milestone achievement in the emancipation of women. In the nineteenth century, liberal humanists such as John Stuart Mill and Harriet Taylor supported the cause of female emancipation, writing in *The Subjection of Women* (1869):

'The principle that regulates the existing social relations between the two sexes — the legal subordination of one sex to the other — is wrong in itself, and now one of the chief hindrances to human improvement; ... it ought to be replaced by a principle of perfect equality, admitting no power or privilege on the one side, nor disability on the other.'

With the arrival of female emancipation in the West, this issue has declined in immediate relevance, but it remains of paramount political importance in countries where women still do not enjoy equal rights.

In Western societies, a more pressing issue for feminists is the question of *equal pay and opportunities for promotion in the workplace*. Using a perspective borrowed from rational-choice theory, some economists maintain that gender inequality is caused by the fact that it is more rational to prioritise the employment of the higher earner. According to this view, it makes sense for men to act as the primary breadwinners, and for women to concentrate on child-rearing (rather than pay others to fulfil this function). However, feminists stress that this argument is valid only because men are paid more than women in the first place: economists are correct to stress the rationality implied in the traditional division of labour, but this ignores the problem of *built-in discrimination*, which feminists see as a primary consequence of patriarchy.

The key issue that feminists seek to address is why women have a differential status within the hierarchical division of labour. In studies of gender inequality in the workplace, sociologists draw a distinction between vertical segregation (which

is characterised by inequality) and horizontal segregation (which is not). In most advanced societies, vertical segregation means that women are able to rise only to a certain point within the hierarchy before they encounter a '**glass ceiling**'. Even where women possess equal skills and qualifications, studies find that they are:

- less likely to gain promotion; and
- less likely to earn as much as men.

Note Think of cases in the news where female employees have taken an employer to court for precisely these reasons.

Feminist ideologies view the sources of gender inequality in very different ways, and there is no agreement about the precise role of patriarchy in the oppression of women. What is clear is that patriarchy is not the only cause of gender inequality:

- Vertical segregation is also explained by the fact that, as latecomers in the labour market (both manual and non-manual), women have had less opportunity to get hold of the better jobs. Hence men remain in control of the top jobs, and can use their superior status within organisations to form networks designed to defend their privileged position.
- Horizontal segregation can be explained by the fact that women have often taken up jobs in new growth areas, for example in the white-collar sector. The growth of routine non-manual jobs in this sector has absorbed more women than men, who often remain tied to or identified with more traditional occupations.

Not all feminist theorists advocate absolute equality with men. For many radical feminists, the idea of equality implies equivalence — something they reject as undesirable. This ambivalence stems from the fact that radical feminists celebrate *feminine* modes of thought and behaviour as positive alternatives to male social and cultural forms. They do not wish to 'level' the differences between men and women, only to eliminate the ideological and social-structural barriers that serve to perpetuate the domination of male social and cultural forms.

3 *Liberal feminism*

Liberal feminists are motivated by two key ideological concerns: individualism and formal equality. Unlike radical feminists, liberal feminists advocate a reformist agenda to correct historic patterns of discrimination. Liberal feminist ideas entered mainstream politics in the post-war era, with the publication of groundbreaking works in Europe and North America demanding equal rights for women. This followed the *de facto* entry of large numbers of educated women into the workforce and the decline of traditional conservative theories of male authority and male superiority.

3.1 Formal equality

Liberals traditionally advocate formal equality, namely that all individuals have a right to equal treatment. As political liberals, liberal feminists argue that women should have equal recognition as citizens, and an equal formal right to personal development and advancement: for too long women have been denied full political and legal equality with men, which has held them back. In this sense, there is a *utilitarian* dimension to liberal feminism: prejudice against women has a detrimental impact on society as a whole because if 50% of society are denied equal rights to develop their talents and skills, e.g. through access to education, then these talents and skills will be lost to the community, undermining social and cultural progress.

The principal goal of liberal feminist activists has been to promote changes in the law outlawing discrimination, particularly in the workplace. An example of this is the Sex Discrimination Act 1975 in the UK, which formalised women's rights to equal treatment in the workplace on the basis of merit rather than sex/gender.

One of the strengths of liberal feminism is that it avoids the sectarian ideology of more radical feminist agendas. This has allowed liberal feminist ideas to enter the political mainstream, and to adopt a reasoned critique of traditional forms of prejudice and discrimination. However, liberal feminists have been criticised for being too concerned with the welfare and status of middle-class women in the West. Similarly, they are criticised for contributing to the preservation of the private/public distinction: by focusing exclusively on the rights of the individual, they fail to see how patriarchy operates through the social construction of gender and the social-structural constraints on full female emancipation.

3.2 Individualism

Liberal feminists also stress the sovereignty of the individual: no person should be coerced unless it is to prevent harm being caused to another. Liberals believe that society is simply an 'aggregation of individuals': it is false to draw ontological distinctions between the community as a group and the individuals who comprise it. Although this reflects a nineteenth-century bias towards atomism, this individualist perspective separates individuals from predetermined social and cultural roles, and is for this reason important for liberal feminists.

The liberal-feminist belief in individualism also reflects the liberal commitment to *autonomy*, although many liberal feminists seek a form of autonomy that avoids stereotypically masculine traits such as toughness, independence and self-sufficiency, which may be inhospitable to women who often thrive by creating and sustaining supportive relations with women.

For liberals the point of feminism is to challenge the traditional control exercised by men over women's individual choices and to advance female social mobility, not to challenge the existing structure of patriarchy. Hence the normative goals of formal equality and individual choice remain the primary aims of liberal feminism, which has done much to advance the position of women in the rich industrialised nations of the West in the post-war period as more women have made the transition from purely domestic labour to participation in the labour force.

Critics of liberal feminism such as Marilyn Friedman, author of *Autonomy, Gender, Politics*, insist that, while women should aspire to autonomy, they should nevertheless avoid emulating entirely the Western cultural perception of autonomy as 'something to be achieved by erecting a wall of rights and privileges' between individuals. Feminists should, she insists, embrace a 'relational approach' to autonomy, one that posits humans as *social* beings as well as individual agents.

4 Radical feminism

Radical feminism grew out of the 'second wave' of feminist activism in the 1970s, among those who no longer believed that inclusion into the formal universal political structures of liberal–capitalist society could address — let alone resolve — the specific problems experienced by women in patriarchal cultures. As Gills, Howie and Munford (editors of *Third Wave Feminism: A Critical Exploration*) argue, 'disappointed by the fact that substantive change had not followed on from the modification of political structures, second wave feminists concerned themselves with broader social relations'.

This led to a turn away from the 'universal' condition of women (the idea that all women share a set of common interests and moral claims) in favour of more differentiated, exclusive approaches. It also led to a rejection of humanism as a paradigm for women's liberation and empowerment because, by advocating the assimilation of women into the existing male world, liberal humanism effectively defines 'femininity' as the primary vehicle of women's oppression in the first place. The result has been a radical critique of patriarchy, and the search for positive gynocentric alternatives to the existing sex/gender system. Radical feminism is a distinctive ideology, which blames the exploitation of women directly on men, and seeks to address this problem by focusing on the role of patriarchy in social reproduction.

Unlike liberal feminists, radical feminists focus on the role of patriarchy in the family. From early childhood onwards, they argue, girls are socialised into subordinate gender roles and channelled into occupations reflecting their subordinate status in society as a whole. If patriarchal domination is to be eliminated, then the social organisation of the traditional nuclear family must be addressed and restructured, or simply avoided. Only in this way can women achieve emancipation and develop their own ways of being outside the prevailing framework of patriarchal domination.

Going beyond liberal feminism, therefore, radical feminists find in women's bodies and in women's cultural practices alternatives to the 'phallocentric' world of violence, selfishness and competitiveness. This does not involve a repudiation of femininity in an attempt to adapt to a masculine world, but its celebration. As Professor Iris Marion Young (1949–2006) argued, for radical gynocentric feminists, women's oppression consists of the devaluation and repression of women's nature and female activity by the patriarchal culture.

Note For some radical feminists the obvious solution to male domination is to recognise that women cannot achieve emancipation as long as they are economically and culturally dependent on men.

4.1 Radical–separatist feminism

Separatist feminists maintain that the institution of patriarchy is so ingrained that women should avoid all political alliances that depend on male support or assistance. This is not because 'all men are evil', but because male consciousness of gender is unavoidably imbued with the assumption of male superiority: because men are socialised to be dominant, they cannot help treating women as natural subordinates.

As a result, male and female interests are mutually antagonistic, and women should organise outside the framework of patriarchal society. Some radical–separatist feminists also advocate sexual independence from men. In practice this entails a celebration of female homosociality and homosexuality, and some radical–separatists emphasise alternative reproductive techniques as a means for reducing dependence on men.

This emphasis on separateness alarms not just conservatives but also liberal feminists, who are anxious to avoid utopian thinking and who reject radical alternatives to the male/female family as unworkable. However, sociological research into alternative households shows that responsible motherhood and parenting are perfectly possible without male role models.

4.2 Radical–cultural feminism

For radical–cultural feminists, gynocentrism makes sense because it asserts the need for women to achieve autonomy without identifying with masculinist culture's equation of humanity with rationality. This has led some radical feminists to suggest that male and female cultures are fundamentally distinct. As Kate Millett argues, 'because of our social circumstances, male and female are really two cultures and their life experiences are utterly different'. However, Millett emphasises not just the *distinctiveness* but the *superiority* of female social and cultural forms over male social and cultural forms. This can be seen in the following examples:

- Women depend more on intuition than on pure intellect, which allows for a more subjective form of understanding and an empathic way of communicating.
- Women are more inclined towards cooperation than competition, which is less antagonistic and less likely to result in conflict.
- Women are more inclined to share and create supportive communities.
- Women are more spontaneous than hierarchical and ordered.

From this perspective, Millett and others seek to focus on the ways in which female social and cultural forms are transmitted, not necessarily in competition with existing male forms, but as alternative criteria of social and political organisation. However, this has led to accusations of 'essentialism' from liberal critics, who suggest that, by focusing on what is specific to women, radical–cultural feminists locate the 'essential attributes' of femininity in the same source as biological determinists, namely the female mode of reproductive consciousness, e.g. giving, nurturing and mothering.

4.3 Radical–libertarian feminism

Representatives of this branch of feminism take a more extreme view of gender, arguing that the only effective solution to the problem of patriarchy is to eliminate gender difference as the cause of inequality. Radical–libertarian feminists propose abolishing 'gender-specific' codes, i.e. the criteria (dress/mannerisms/body language) that differentiate 'active-assertive' males from 'passive-submissive' females. In this respect, some **'Amazon' feminists** stress that women are discouraged from thinking they can fulfil tasks traditionally associated with men, including heavy manual labour. They argue that women can achieve sexual equality only by discarding this assumption.

In its most extreme form, this amounts to a call for **androgyny**, where the physical distinction between men and women is reduced through non-gendered socialisation. Radical–libertarian feminists believe that this can be achieved if men and women embrace the positive attributes of both masculinity and femininity — not in a physical sense, but as a recognition of the positive dimensions of both masculinity and femininity.

Once the *cultural determinants* of gender identity are addressed, men and women could become emotionally and physically more alike, rather than conforming to stereotyped and exaggerated expressions of masculinity and femininity promoted by the advertising industry.

This critique leads in the opposite direction to gynocentric approaches, avoiding the trap of rejecting all masculine cultural forms as negative. Gender is, for radical libertarians, just a construct, which is easily transcended through alternative forms of socialisation. However, the radical–libertarian critique should not be confused with post-feminist approaches, which hold that radical feminism's denial of the growth-promoting dimensions of masculinity is ultimately counter-productive.

5 *Marxist feminism*

Some commentators have argued that there is a natural affinity between socialism and feminism in view of the fact that women in particular, and the working class in general, are oppressed groups in society. This view is contested by radical feminists, who view patriarchy, not class, as the primary issue. They stress that there is an inherent tension between feminism and Marxism on the basis that feminists prioritise gender divisions, while Marxists prioritise class struggle.

> *Note* Marxist feminists identify class rather than patriarchy as the primary category in social–scientific analysis. For Marxist feminists, the category 'patriarchy' obscures the distinction between the human capacity and necessity to create a sexual world, and the actual oppressive ways in which sexual worlds have been organised, e.g. under capitalism.

5.1 Class and gender

The earliest attempt to reconcile the problems of class and female emancipation can be found in the work of Friedrich Engels. In *The Origins of the Family, Private Property and the State*, Engels argued that women are effectively part of the 'reserve army of labour', which can be used to supplement the male labour force under conditions of increased production. Marxists point out that women's emancipation in the capitalist system has come at a high price: although women have benefited from the freedom associated with employment, most households have become dependent on two incomes rather than one, and households also pay twice as much in taxation.

Engels also argued that women play a vital supportive role in the maintenance of the capitalist system by providing a secure domestic environment for men, by mitigating the negative impact of harsh working conditions and by rearing the next generation of workers.

This view was adopted by orthodox Marxists, who argued that gender relations would eventually be transformed under socialist 'relations of production'. However, the example of the former communist states does not support this view. In the Soviet Union, women were subjected to the double burden of full-time labour and homemaking, while men continued to occupy the highest positions in the hierarchical division of labour. Women took up jobs traditionally performed by men, but this did not alter the underlying structure of patriarchal domination.

More recent Marxist feminists have tried to reconcile the issues of class domination and patriarchy by locating both problems within a broader critique of capitalism as a mode of production that '**interpellates**' (incorporates) individuals into the system. This process of ideological incorporation occurs at both a material and an ideological level:

- At the material level, capitalism transforms raw materials into finished goods by using human labour and other productive forces.
- At an ideological level, the system functions by transforming the way individuals relate to the actual conditions of their existence by representing reality in a distorted form.

According to Marxist feminists the subordination of women in capitalist society is a logical correlate to the subordination of labour to the rule of capital. The main difference is that women are subjected to domination at two levels — first at the level of class, second at the level of gender. In this sense, gender becomes a subordinate category of class, which is determined by the relation of individuals to the means of production.

5.2 Ideological integration

Since the pioneering work of Gramsci, who defined hegemony as 'domination by consent', Marxists have sought to understand the longevity of capitalism by explaining its mode of ideological integration: it is not enough for the bourgeoisie to rule; rather, it must rule with the *consent* of the ruled by incorporating workers into the dominant values of the ruling class. For Marxist feminists, women are integrated into the values of the capitalist system in two ways:

- On one level, they falsely identify with the hegemonic values of possessive individualism. Women enter the workforce to carry out routine labour tasks that men either will not or cannot perform themselves. Through acquiring limited income and status, women are incorporated ideologically: they adopt the values of the system, and aspire to have the things capitalism produces, emulating middle-class women and celebrities. At the same time, their success serves as a further incentive for men to work hard in order to impress women, maintain their own status and acquire consumer goods (this is particularly important as women now constitute more than 50% of the labour force in some developed societies).
- On another level, women are encouraged to internalise patriarchal values and beliefs that acknowledge their changing role as mothers and workers, but that nevertheless still privilege the authority and rule of men within the hierarchical division of labour. Women are incited to achieve social mobility as a substitute for male workers — especially in the service and retail sectors — but are still expected to conform to the pattern of the traditional nuclear family in order to reproduce the patriarchal structure of society and to rear the next generation of workers.

One merit of this theoretical reconciliation of the twin categories, class and patriarchy, is that it acknowledges the advances made by women in capitalist societies but still stresses women's subordinate role. Another merit is that it avoids turning patriarchy into an 'essential', invariant category. However, critics suggest that Marxist feminism oversimplifies patriarchy: by collapsing male domination into class domination, the problem of patriarchy is transformed into a function of capitalism. This fails to take into account patriarchal forms of domination before capitalism, and the fact that patriarchy is most prevalent today in pre-industrial societies.

6 *Postmodern feminism*

For many radical feminists, attempts to theorise a universal condition of womanhood or femininity fails because these categories cannot possibly capture the heterogeneous experience of women in a variety of cultural and political contexts. This dissatisfaction has led to the emergence of a 'third wave' of feminist theory, incorporating a **postmodern** perspective, where the subjective knowledge and experience of women in localised struggles for recognition and emancipation are detached from both a humanist perspective of liberal feminism and the materialist perspective of Marxist feminism. This reflects the 'postmodern turn' in the humanities and social sciences, based on a rejection of liberal Enlightenment narratives of progress and modernity.

The impact of postmodern ideas on feminist ideology can be seen in the way some feminists now reject the liberal assumption that reform can and must lead to a more egalitarian society.

Whereas liberal feminists assume that progress towards universal female emancipation is possible, postmodernists are sceptical about the possibility of real change. In this respect, postmodern feminists reject the liberal–rationalist notion of 'linear progress' (the prevailing idea that history is moving in a single, progressive direction) as a male concept, reflecting the now redundant perspective of eighteenth-century European male writers.

The premise of postmodern feminism is that no single theoretical outlook can adequately explain the position of women in late capitalist societies. Just as postmodern philosophers and sociologists reject the universalising claims of 'grand theory' in favour of localised perspectives, postmodern feminists argue that the experience of different women is sufficiently distinctive to make even core concepts such as patriarchy highly questionable.

This perspective is epitomised by Judith Butler, author of *Gender Trouble*, who argues that essentialist definitions of women should be replaced by genealogical narratives reflecting the cultural construction of femininities as *historic series of overlapping phenomena*. Rather than treat women as a single group (and female emancipation as a single historic cause), postmodern feminists emphasise *multiplicity* and *diversity*. Once the demand for a universal solution to women's oppression by men is abandoned, it becomes possible to view the condition of different groups of women as temporary and contingent rather than final or definite.

Critics of this perspective argue that, while postmodernists are correct to emphasise the importance of different women's experience, by abandoning (a) the rational assumption of progress and (b) a universalist framework for political action, postmodern feminists risk losing the normative driving force that has traditionally propelled the movement for women's emancipation. Liberal feminists criticise the retreat from methodological individualism, which places the individual at the centre of social–scientific explanation; Marxist feminists criticise the retreat from collectivism, which has historically enabled working-class women (and men) to challenge bourgeois hegemony.

Yet despite these criticisms, postmodern feminists insist that the goal of third-wave feminism is to reclaim the struggle against women's oppression for a new generation by focusing on *identity* and *difference*. As Alison Stone, author of *An Introduction to Feminist Philosophy*, argues, essentialism fails because, although it enables women to identify with a common cause (femininity), any strategy that reaffirms 'fictitious commonalities amongst women cannot be expected to facilitate effective action in a world where women do not really have any common characteristics or experiences'. For this reason, feminists such as Alison Stone and Iris Marion Young classify women not as a definable 'group' with a conscious or definite identity, but as a 'series', whose members are 'unified passively through their actions being constrained and organised by particular structures and constellations of material objects'.

7 *Post-feminism*

One of the implications of post-feminist theory is that feminism as a new social movement happened in the 1960s and 1970s, that it achieved many (but not all) of its goals, and that certain types of radical feminism seem to result in utopianism. But does this mean that post-feminism is a revisionist ideology — that post-feminists have abandoned the struggle for women's emancipation in the face of the neoconservative backlash? Or is post-feminism an exercise in consolidation, allowing feminists to take stock of the significant changes in gender relations and political reforms in the advanced societies of the West in the post-war period?

Whereas postmodern feminists call for a recognition of the evolution of femininity and the diversity of female identities, post-feminists not only recognise the weakness of essentialist categories but seek to reclaim and re-legitimise dimensions of women's identity and experience, such as domesticity, consumerism, motherhood and pornography, that are traditionally frowned upon or rejected by radical feminists and socialist feminists as products of patriarchal oppression in capitalist society.

Critics of post-feminism maintain that it substitutes culture and lifestyle issues for the serious social and political issues raised by radical and Marxist feminists. By eschewing direct political organisation and engagement, post-feminists (and, to a lesser extent, postmodern feminists) have lost sight of the need for continued struggle and vigilance against a possible anti-feminist backlash, for example, in the continuing political conflict over abortion in the United States.

However, defenders of post-feminism such as Judith Stacey suggest that it is not meant to indicate the 'death of the women's movement but to describe the simultaneous incorporation, revision, and depoliticisation of many of the central goals of second wave feminism'. In this sense, it is not a submission to sexism or anti-feminism but an *apolitical* incorporation and continuation of feminist goals by other means. Although many post-feminists take a relaxed attitude to issues such as pornography and avoid political correctness, post-feminism represents a continuing dialogue with second-wave feminism based on a continued presumption of the importance of sexual equality *and* a recognition of the achievements of feminist struggles.

Note Some radical feminists argue that post-feminism constitutes an acknowledgement of the failure of the women's movement to radically alter the structure of patriarchy in capitalist society.

Key terms and concepts

Amazon feminists	Sub-group of feminists who focus on the physical equality of men and women and oppose gender-role stereotypes
Androgyny	Condition where individuals display characteristics of both sexes
Biological determinism	Belief that an individual's destiny is determined by inherited biological criteria such as sex
Gender	Sexual identity as expressed through social and cultural distinctions
'Glass ceiling'	Expression denoting the artificial limits placed on female promotion beyond a certain level in the hierarchical division of labour
Interpellation	The inducement and incorporation of individuals into a system of power relations
Patriarchy	Male domination; system of government based on rule by senior men
Postmodernism	Approach to politics and social science that rejects the Enlightenment belief in reason and the inevitability of progress
Separatism	Branch of radical feminism that emphasises the cultural differences between men and women and the need for women to work outside the framework of patriarchal society
Sex	The inherited biological features that differentiate men and women

8 Ecologism

1 Introduction

Ecology and environmentalism are important topics in Unit 4B in the Edexcel and AQA examination papers. Questions refer to the ecological view of nature and the implications of this view for human societies, the differences between rival branches of ecological theory, and the relevance of traditional political categories for green politics. You should also be aware of the impact of climate change and environmentalism on mainstream political debate, and the links between climate change and neoliberal globalisation.

Ecologism is concerned not just with political ideas and beliefs but also with the interaction between human societies and the natural environment. Ecologists view nature as an interconnected whole, *embracing both the human and non-human world*. Although there are a variety of different schools of ecological thought, an overriding theme uniting all ecologists is concern for the negative impact of industrialisation on the natural environment.

For ecologists, the traditional left/right binary in politics is redundant. They argue that 'industrialism' in both its capitalist and socialist forms has become a kind of super-ideology that obscures the real impact of unconstrained growth, rapid urbanisation, overpopulation and climate change on the earth's fragile ecology. **Industrialism** is a consequence of the **anthropocentrism** inherent in ideologies of unlimited growth, which are based on the misguided belief that the natural world exists exclusively for human use and enjoyment and has no value independent of its utility for the human race.

Note Ecologists view both capitalism and socialism as examples of industrialism, which is based on the indefensible logic of growth without end.

Ecologists have formed tactical alliances with socialists, anarchists and feminists, but reject economistic, growth-oriented ideologies such as liberal capitalism and state socialism. Both liberal capitalism and state socialism remain committed to a nineteenth-century vision of 'ever further development', which ecologists see as unsustainable and morally indefensible because it ignores the finite nature of resources such as oil and the dependence of human civilisation on the natural environment.

For 'deep' ecologists in particular, human exploitation of nature is precipitating an irreversible crisis in environment/society relations, which is exacerbated by the refusal of Europe, North America and Japan to countenance any reduction in their standard of living and consumption of natural resources.

Key issues and debates
- the challenge to anthropocentrism;
- the distinction between 'shallow' and 'deep' ecology;
- the distinction between ecologism and environmentalism;
- the link between ecologism and feminism;
- the link between ecologism and anarchism; and
- green politics.

2 Core ideas of ecologism

2.1 Ecology and diversity

From an ecological perspective nature is viewed as an interconnected whole. Ecologists argue that the relationship between different species is 'web-like' rather than hierarchical, i.e. mankind does not exist at the apex of some imaginary hierarchy, but is dependent on other ecosystems for survival. Ecologists are also concerned with the diversity and complexity of the natural and social world, and the problematic way in which humans attempt to understand it.

Humans have traditionally adopted a reductionist approach to science, preferring to study natural and social phenomena by placing everything in small, intelligible categories. Ecologists argue that, by subsuming reality into discrete categories, we fail to identify how economic, social and natural–environmental processes interact in a complex **ecosystem**. They also criticise the tendency towards simplification (e.g. dependence on a few species of grass to provide nutrition), which undermines the capacity of ecosystems to withstand shocks, and industrial modes of production, which destroy biodiversity and make ecosystems more vulnerable to collapse.

There are, however, differences between 'shallow' and 'deep' ecologism, which must be clearly understood:

- *Shallow ecologists* advocate environmental protection, conservation and sustainability, but seek to do so within the framework of the existing industrial system. They continue to place human needs above those of nature as a whole, and work *within* the constraints of the political system by pushing a pragmatic, reformist agenda. Shallow ecologists have achieved limited goals through accommodation with the existing system, accepting that mainstream politicians are not only slow to accept the findings of environmental research, but also vulnerable to electoral pressures from voters whose key preference is increased consumption.
- *Deep ecologists* assume a more radical 'ecocentric' position, giving priority to the preservation of ecological balance rather than to human welfare. They argue that, as long as the anthropocentric ideas and beliefs of industrialism remain dominant, humanity will continue on its present course towards environmental catastrophe. Hence the existing system itself has to change. Deep ecologism has suffered from negative stereotyping because some of its advocates have assumed irrational, mystical or even anti-humanist views.

The Kyoto Protocol on carbon emissions, ratified by all the main polluting countries except the United States, demonstrates the potential of moderate, pragmatic **environmentalism** over deep ecologism. Although the protocol has not solved the problem of global warming caused by greenhouse gases (damage is already far advanced and its consequences unforeseeable), it at least provides a framework for international cooperation, exerting moral and political pressure on polluting countries to develop more responsible energy policies.

2.2 Anti-anthropocentrism

From a deep ecological perspective, traditional ideologies have an anthropocentric bias: they privilege the status and welfare of humans in the world, and celebrate mankind's mastery over nature, but completely ignore the fact that humans are a species of animal and thus subject to the same ecological laws as other living organisms.

At the heart of deep ecologism is a critique of the 'instrumental' rationality of man's exploitative relationship with the natural environment. Ecologists insist that this **instrumentalism**, which reduces man's relationship with nature to technical or pragmatic considerations, eliminates the possibility of normativity and reduces the definition of the 'moral community' to human beings alone. Deep ecologists insist that nature has an intrinsic moral value, regardless of whether it is useful for human ends. What

is required is an alternative approach to economic development, which extends the definition of the 'moral community' by taking into account not only existing human needs, but also:

- the welfare of the non-human and inanimate world;
- the finite nature of resources;
- the needs of future generations;
- the welfare of 'subaltern' groups negatively affected by environmental injustice; and
- sustainable development.

Radical ecologists such as Kenneth Boulding (author of *Ecodynamics: A New Theory of Societal Evolution*) maintain that the earth should be seen as a self-contained system, a 'tiny sphere, closed, limited, crowded, and hurtling through space to unknown destinations'. This self-regulating natural system, which the environmental scientist James Lovelock famously termed 'Gaia', cannot be reduced to the sum of its parts. It is, rather, an intrinsically dynamic and interconnected web of relations within which there is no inherent dividing line between organic and non-organic phenomena, and no absolute division between the human and non-human realms.

Deep ecologists also argue that it is no longer possible to regard the earth as an infinite reservoir, an infinite source of inputs and an infinite 'cesspool' for outputs, e.g. pollution of the oceans. When mankind was still a relatively small species, it could pollute with impunity, given the capacity of the natural environment to absorb limited despoliation. Now that this is no longer possible, due to overpopulation and resource depletion, humans must learn to co-exist within the earth's ecosystem as a whole, and face up to the problem of *material entropy*, which human activities create.

Entropy is a measure of the unavailability of energy, but is also understood by environmental scientists as the tendency of natural structures to disperse and disintegrate. The separation process in the extraction and utilisation of resources impairs the adaptive potential/resilience of natural capital (resources) over time, leading to collapsing support for human societies and economies. In ideological terms, Boulding argues:

'Man is finally going to have to face the fact that he is a biological system living in an ecological system, and that his survival… is going to depend on his developing symbiotic relationships of a closed-cycle character with all the other elements and populations of the world of ecological systems. What this means, in effect, is that all the other forms of life will have to be domesticated, even if on wildlife preserves.'

This arresting view has several implications:
- anthropocentric perspectives are no longer viable;
- economic growth must be linked to **sustainability**;
- mankind must accept the reality of resource scarcity;
- there must be limits to pollution and population growth; and
- consumption patterns have to change.

The most obvious example of unsustainable development is the use of carbon-based fossil fuels, particularly oil and natural gas, the remainder of which is concentrated in a handful of geopolitically unstable locations. Ecologists argue that the long-term implications of industrial pollution, e.g. climate change, are unknown, and the risks incalculable. What is clear, however, is that existing patterns of population growth are unsustainable, particularly in the developing world. Mankind should embrace alternative technologies to balance the twin needs of growth and sustainability.

Deep ecologists take this critique one step further, and argue that the goals of continued growth and sustainable development are contradictory. They suggest that the human preoccupation with growth has resulted in overdevelopment in rich countries and environmental injustice and underdevelopment in poor countries.

2.3 Environmental ethics

The main conclusion of the ecological critique of industrialism is that mankind has to develop new environmental ethics embracing the human, non-human and inanimate world. One of the main priorities of the Environmental Justice Movement is to increase awareness of our moral obligation to future generations. Ecologists argue that humans tend to think in terms only of their own lifespan, making it difficult for them to see that they have an obligation to future generations. Likewise, people tend to think in terms of their own communities and nations, making it difficult to think of issues in global terms. Yet environmental problems affect *all* the earth's inhabitants, and territorial borders are no defence against man-made problems like global warming. It is this limited understanding of the implications of mankind's activities which ecologists seek to challenge.

> *Note* Most people are now aware of the problems caused by climate change and environmental destruction, but are reluctant to draw relevant inferences for their own behaviour.

The key ethical goals of the **ecology** movement can be summarised as follows:
- egalitarianism (equal distribution of wealth);
- internationalism (the capacity to 'think globally');
- democratisation (allowing people a voice in economic decisions that will affect them); and
- moral autonomy (increasing the capacity of individuals and communities to act rationally).

3 Environmentalism

The term 'environmentalism' is often confused with the term 'ecologism', but environmentalists are concerned with a more limited range of issues. In principle, environmentalism deals with the *effects* rather than the causes of environmental problems, while ecologism is a fully fledged ideology in its own right, which opposes productivist ideologies as incompatible with sustainable development. Environmentalists assume a humanist stance towards the existing system: it is essential to work within the framework of political and economic system if one wants to achieve limited change.

The point of environmentalist campaigns is to limit the impact of environmental 'bads' on *human* life, rather than nature as a whole. Environmentalists continue to operate within the prevailing framework of industrialism, where human economic and cultural development remains detached from its ecological context. They are concerned with three main issues:
- limiting the negative impact of environmental issues on human life;
- wildlife and conservation issues; and
- defence of rural communities and traditional ways of life.

Environmentalists are also often conservative in outlook, but maintain that right-wing politicians have for too long approached environmentalism as if it were an invention of the left, and as if there were no serious environmental concerns. As conservatives, they believe that the solution to environmental problems lies with individual responsibility: the more individuals renege on this responsibility, the more likely governments will be forced to accept radical or totalitarian solutions promoted by left-wing ecologists. Like conservatives, many conservationists defend property rights, arguing that the best way to protect scarce resources is to promote a link between ownership and responsibility. This amounts to a pragmatic argument based on market value:

If resources are becoming scarcer, then the logical response is to ensure that their increased value to humanity is reflected in their value in the marketplace; then and only then will companies have a rational incentive to change their behaviour.

This argument has many merits, and has been adopted in political strategies such as carbon-credit trading, where polluting countries negotiate quotas on maximum emissions and trade surpluses wherever possible. However, ecologists argue that such strategies fail to address the real issue, namely mankind's instrumental relationship with nature. Conservationism is limited in its goals, and although conservation groups now exercise some influence over rural and environmental policies, their lack of radicalism means that underlying ecological questions are not addressed.

Note Many conservative environmentalists believe that defence of the natural environment can best be achieved by encouraging responsible ownership and conservation of natural resources and wildlife habitats.

4 *Ecosocialism*

In *From Red to Green,* the former East German Marxist Rudolf Bahro argued that socialists tend to reduce all the problems of resources to a socio-economic level, arguing that the system of capitalist reproduction alone is at fault. Yet the survival of the human race depends not just on egalitarian distribution, but also on maintaining the unwieldy structures of industrialism. The real choice for socialists is, he argued, between the 'peaceful dismantling of the huge structures we have built and the collapse of the whole system, with even more disastrous consequences for future generations than for ourselves'.
The shift from economic justice to ecological rationality in ecosocialist ideology is an important and inevitable consequence of the collapse of productivist state socialism

Note Ecosocialists seek to reconcile ecocentric and anthropocentric thinking by arguing that social justice is an essential precondition for achieving ecological goals.

in the USSR and Eastern Europe, where rapid industrialisation caused severe environmental damage in the race to 'overtake capitalism without catching up'. The core thesis of ecosocialism is that *capitalism* is the source of all ecological problems, not simply because it is based on uncontrolled growth ('growth without reason'), but because growth itself has become a substitute for a more egalitarian distribution of resources in the industrialised world.

According to David Pepper, author of *Eco-socialism: From Deep Ecology to Social Justice,* the fundamental point of ecosocialism is that mankind must proceed towards ecology from social justice and not the other way around. The main political issues facing the world are environmental catastrophe *and* inequality: unless restructured and restrained, global capitalism will grow at an ever faster rate before eventually undermining the fragile ecological infrastructure upon which it depends. State socialism arguably collapsed due to bureaucratic mismanagement, corruption and environmental devastation; for ecosocialists, the global economy is equally vulnerable unless the rapacious character of neoliberal capitalism is addressed.

Liberal optimists believe that increasing environmental degradation will be enough to push world leaders towards innovative solutions, by reducing either consumption or the global population. This will then encourage a higher degree of equality in the distribution of material resources, promoting social justice and ending poverty. Ecosocialists insist that such idealism is based on 'petty-bourgeois utopianism'.

According to David Ransom, author of the article 'Red and Green: eco-socialism comes of age' in *New Internationalist* magazine, the dilemma facing mankind is to 'grow or blow'. 'The destruction is compounded,' he writes, 'because it must either grow or blow: it cannot contain itself. It is self-destructive, too, shot through with contradictions which [will] make it blow precisely because it grows like some force-fed hothouse vegetable.' Why is this the case?

For Ransom, capitalism inflates profits, deflates wages and increases inequality, fuelling a recurrent crisis between production and consumption. As markets expand and contract, capitalist firms move on to new forms of production to maintain profits. This occurs without regard for the finite nature of resources, or for the utility of the consumer goods produced. The system is irrational because it creates new needs where they previously did not exist, in the process wasting precious resources.

The most obvious consequences of this are the explosion of consumer debt in the West and the massive expansion of industrial pollution in China as the principal location of global manufacturing in the post-Cold War era.

The primary target of ecosocialist activism is corporate capitalism, which, in an attempt to maintain the system of private ownership for private profit, appropriates and subverts 'green' ideology for its own purpose. Ecosocialists such as David Pepper insist that 'green consumerism' is simply an alternative source of profitability for the capitalist economy, and that mainstream green movements have 'become counter-revolutionary by not challenging the material basis of our society but becoming part of it conveying the idea that it *can* continue in a very basic way. Thus consumerism is acceptable if it is "green" consumerism and part of "green" capitalism.'

5   *Ecoanarchism*

Anarchism, according to George Woodcock, author of *Anarchism: A History of Libertarian Ideas and Movements*, is a 'doctrine which contends that government is the source of most of our social troubles and that there are viable alternative forms of voluntary organisation'. Ecology, on the other hand, is concerned with understanding the interdependence between human social systems and nature. At what level do these two ideologies intersect?

The answer lies in their mutual rejection of the modern industrial state — particularly its capitalist variant — as an *unnatural* and *unworkable* system of social reproduction.

According to ecoanarchists, the industrial state is dependent on structures that dwarf human communities, rendering obsolete natural forms of regulation and control. This dehumanising system creates the need for a modern state, in order to micro-manage the population in accordance with the needs of the system itself. In this way, education ceases to be concerned with cultivating intelligent and autonomous individuals, becoming instead a means to produce 'useful citizens'. Education robs children of their natural creativity, and moulds them instead into obedient drones.

Ecocentric anarchists thus reject the traditional emphasis, within individualist and collectivist anarchism, on the state as the root of all evil. The real issue is not the contradiction between authority and autonomy, but man's relation of domination towards nature, which is reproduced in the political structures that govern human societies. Ecological imbalance, authoritarianism, injustice, war and racism are all direct and inevitable consequences of industrial civilisation.

Note For ecoanarchists the ecological problems facing the earth stem from mankind's urge to dominate nature, which is further reflected in the hierarchical and authoritarian structure of the state.

There are important distinctions within ecoanarchism, based on the extent to which groups accept or reject existing urbanised industrial civilisation. The main strands of ecoanarchist ideology are threefold:

- *Green* anarchism is often confused with primitivism, which advocates a return to small village communities. However, not all green anarchists seek to return to a primitive way of life. Like anarcho–syndicalists (who are often unjustly labelled Luddites), green anarchists believe in applying advanced technology in an ecologically friendly way, and do not see an inherent conflict between technology and biodiversity. 'Viridian Greens', for example, see advantages in key technologies, especially those that offer the human species the possibility of transforming itself into something more ecologically rational.
- *Ecoanarchism* is a branch of anarchism that focuses on the environmental dimension of anarchist theory. American ecoanarchists such as Murray Bookchin and John Zerzan are concerned with the question of 'social ecology', based on the idea that nature and society are interlinked by evolution into a single nature comprised of two dimensions — first ('biotic') nature, and second ('human') nature. First nature refers to the natural world as humans find it, made up of living beings and inanimate matter. Second nature refers to the adaptive environment that humans create to support their mode of existence.
- *Primitivism* is a radical variant of ecocentric anarchism, advocating a return to pre-industrial society. Primitivists believe that industrial states produce oppressive structures through the hierarchisation and division of labour, and that technology has negative implications. Some forms of primitivism question civilisation itself, suggesting that humans return to a non-urbanised form of life, free from the all-pervasive structures of authority, surveillance and control. Like some green anarchists, they believe that the optimal form of social organisation is the village community, in which individuals can co-exist in a state of balance and harmony with the environment.

Yet critics of ecoanarchism point to a contradiction in ecoanarchist reasoning: while calling for a return to pre-industrial forms of social organisation, and for the abolition of traditional authority, ecoanarchists fail to see that the preservation of harmonious communities and maintenance of sustainable development may in fact be dependent on *conservative* institutions such as patriarchy and hierarchy, which reproduce stable human structures and practices over time. It is the *atomistic* bias of libertarian thinking that undermines the capacity of human communities to maintain a balance between continuity and change, robbing individuals of consistent value-orientations and stable horizons.

6 *Ecofeminism*

Ecofeminists hold that the survival of (human) life on the planet is dependent on the abolition of patriarchal norms and values, which legitimise the destructive tendencies of industrial capitalism. According to Maria Mies and Vandana Shiva, authors of *Ecofeminism*, this system 'emerged, is built upon, and maintains itself through the colonisation of women, of "foreign" peoples and their lands; and of nature, which it is gradually destroying'. From this perspective the ecocentric goals of environmental protection and sustainability are dependent on overcoming the exploitative and oppressive relations between men and women in patriarchal societies.

Note Ecofeminists seek to reconcile the critique of patriarchy with the critique of industrialism, linking exploitation of nature with male oppression of women.

Whereas ecosocialists are concerned with the connection between equality and ecology, ecofeminists regard the oppression of women and nature as interconnected. From an ecofeminist perspective, there is a clear and obvious parallel between male domination in society (as expressed through the institution of patriarchy) and mankind's domination of nature (as expressed through the uncritical and unregulated exploitation of natural resources).

The underlying assumption of ecofeminist theory is that nature in its pure form is characterised by feminine virtues, e.g. love, compassion and cooperation. These have been overshadowed by male virtues such as power, authority, technical competence and competitiveness. Ecofeminists also emphasise the superiority of 'female spirituality' over 'male materialism'. Spirituality is celebrated because it encourages self-introspection, ethical reflection and creativity. Materialism, on the other hand, encourages instrumental action, and is epitomised by 'male' subjects such as economics in which the rationale is growth without reason, with little or no regard for the environmental costs of human productive activity.

Ecofeminists emphasise the importance of individual responsibility in bringing about moral and spiritual renewal, and seek to embrace nature as an equal partner, rather than as a field for human material experiments. In this sense, they advocate a complete break with the traditional productivist logic of industrial civilisation, and a return to communities based on mutual respect, compassion and the emancipation of feminine values and modes of living.

David Kronlid, author of *Ecofeminism and Environmental Ethics*, suggests that ecofeminist reasoning challenges traditional ethical thinking in two ways. On the one hand, as ecologists, ecofeminists hold that mankind's relationship with nature constitutes the foundation upon which moral reflection proceeds: anti-anthropocentric reasoning implies that nature needs to be taken into consideration in its own right. On the other hand, as feminists, ecofeminists question whether it is possible to separate reason and emotion in the interests of preserving value-neutrality. In this way, ecofeminism

subordinates reason to context: the individualistic self of liberalism is replaced by a 'social self' shaped by culture and interaction with nature.

Ecofeminist movements thus vary in form between countries, depending on the nature of local struggles and contexts:

- In the industrialised world, ecofeminists challenge the prevailing values of patriarchal capitalism, and seek to foster alternative technologies of living through spiritualism, consciousness-raising and retreat into non-materialist communities.
- In the developing world, ecofeminists are more concerned with maintaining access to vital resources rather than with education or lifestyle issues, reflecting the greater harshness of life for women in traditional patriarchal societies where women (and children) are statistically more likely to fall into poverty and destitution than men.

This reflects the increasing diversity of the women's movement itself in a post-feminist age, in which the Eurocentric and rationalistic ideals of liberal universalism have been displaced by a differentiated, localised approach based on the recognition of cultural and contextual factors.

7 *Green politics*

7.1 Emergence of a green agenda

Contemporary green politics has its origins in the new social movements of the 1960s and 1970s, which emerged in response to the crisis of the Keynesian industrial welfare state ('Fordism'). Fordism was itself a political response to the emergence and development of mass society, which led to the stabilisation of the capitalist system in the post-war era, but also to the increasing commodification and bureaucratisation of social life. Based on a 'rising expectations model', Fordism presupposes unlimited growth and consumption — assumptions that green activists reject because, they argue, population growth, climate change and resource depletion threaten the survival of the human race. According to social scientists, new social movements such as environmentalism and ecologism reflect a search for meaning and authenticity during periods of transition when older forms of integration and representation no longer serve to legitimise unequal distributions of power and resources. Alberto Melucci, author of *Nomads of the Present: Social Movements and Individual Needs in Contemporary Society*, argues that new social movements are political in a different sense of the term: they refuse to play by a set of rules that typically benefits *existing* power-holders. This makes it more difficult for such movements to be co-opted by state actors, allowing them greater potential to challenge power-holders and majority opinion.

Green politics are characterised by *diversity* rather than *unity*. There are numerous types of environmentalist and ecological organisations, each of which attempts to influence national and international policies through specific forms of activism and political participation. Since the 1970s, the maturation of green politics has taken place against the backdrop of debates on climate change and pollution at the end of the 'oil age'. Green activists argue that conventional politicians fail to consider the problem of resource scarcity in their manifesto commitments, which are usually based on the assumption of unlimited growth and consumption. At best, politicians believe that scarcity can be resolved through the price mechanism; at worst, they ignore the problem altogether and remain prisoners to sectional economic interests whose primary goal is profitability.

Note Green movements have to confront the problem that mainstream politicians continue to offer voters the dream of increasing affluence and consumption.

Although the evolution of green politics reflects *international* political trends (the influence of international pressure groups, non-governmental organisations and supra-governmental bodies), the success of *national* green parties and movements depends entirely on the sophistication of local political elites and voters in a range of political contexts:

- In countries such as Sweden and Germany, the Greens have achieved high levels of parliamentary representation, to the point of entering governmental coalitions.
- In contrast, the Green Party in the UK (formerly the Ecology Party) remains at the margins of national politics, partly as a consequence of the winner-takes-all electoral system.
- In developing countries, green movements have less hope of influencing governments, who remain dependent on economic and financial interests, which may be antagonistic to ecological concerns.

From this perspective, although ecological concerns are clearly *universal*, green politics is characterised by a plurality of *local* experiences, which shape and determine the evolution of green agendas in different contexts. For radical green movements, activism and protest are the preferred options, given the prevailing anthropocentric consensus in mainstream party politics.

7.2 Die Grünen in Germany

The German Grünen are often identified as the most important political force in the European ecology movement. The party achieved the highest level of political office when its former leader, Joschka Fischer, became foreign minister in the Red–Green coalition government of Gerhard Schröder. Yet, as James Radcliffe, author of *Green Politics: Dictatorship or Democracy?*, notes, for '*die Grünen* the problems began with the their successful attainment of a degree of power unknown to any other ecology party. Once this had been achieved the divisions that were evident but tolerated began to emerge more significantly'.

Note The formation of the Red–Green coalition in Germany in 1998 demonstrates the potential benefits of green-party participation in the political process; but it also highlights the dangers of achieving high office, which inevitably causes tensions between the parliamentary leadership and the mass party.

These divisions — between the party's realist and fundamentalist wings — reflect the dilemma facing ecology parties that make the transition from new social movement to established political party:

- For the realist wing, the aim is to gain power in order to implement piecemeal changes, e.g. energy taxes. Only by achieving high office, they argue, can outsider groups change anything.
- For the fundamentalist wing, power is only ever a means to a higher end, namely to bring about a sea-change in public consciousness of ecological issues and the contradictions inherent in anthropocentrism.

Die Grünen have also suffered from their own commitment to democracy, which, by promoting organisational transparency, magnifies the splits between different factions. Their accession to power in 1998 in a coalition with the Social Democrats (SPD) temporarily concealed these divisions, but tensions between the parliamentary faction and the party faithful did not disappear.

The SPD–Grünen coalition formed in 1998 gave die Grünen three senior cabinet positions and a number of lower-level posts. Yet the coalition was based ultimately on a deal over the future of Germany's nuclear-power industry, and here the problems began. The SPD — ever mindful of the importance of industry for the German economy — were reluctant to specify a date for the decommissioning of nuclear energy. This policy vagueness was partially compensated for by the charismatic appeal and political skill of Joschka Fischer, who was forced to balance the competing interests of high office with the radical political demands emanating from the left wing of his party. This problem was particularly acute following Germany's participation in NATO's military intervention in Kosovo, which was opposed by radical pacifist elements in the party who rejected the *Realpolitik* of German political establishment.

The impact of government participation on die Grünen has been mixed. On the one hand, entry into the Red–Green coalition enhanced the party's profile as a serious force in national politics. This was aided by the pragmatism of Fischer, who astutely supported Schröder over unpopular decisions. On the other hand, the bitter compromises made by the leadership alienated many core voters (especially the young), precipitating a decline in the party's electoral support. Despite this, die Grünen remain above the 5% hurdle necessary for representation in the Federal parliament.

7.3 Green politics in the UK

The ecology movement in the UK has consistently lagged behind its continental counterparts, and few observers would ever predict the formation of a Red–Green coalition in Westminster. Nevertheless, the progress of the ecology movement in the UK has been noticeable in the last decade, spurred on by debates over climate change and opposition to neoliberal globalisation.

The UK Ecology Party was founded in 1973 in an attempt to promote green issues and transcend the traditional adversarial nature of British politics by adopting radical new policies. One of the key figures of the party (which has traditionally lacked a clear and visible leader) was Jonathon Porritt, who realised that electoral participation was unlikely to yield significant political gains. Yet this strategy has proved successful in the long run, allowing the Green Party to progress from being an outsider pressure group supported only by committed middle-class activists to becoming a national party with representation in local and regional government.

One of the early goals of the Green Party was to promote a decentralisation of political power, leading to a reduction in the influence of Whitehall over the economic and political life of the UK. The party formed alliances with radical left-of-centre and pacifist groups (including Greenpeace and CND), and cultivated a 'deep green' opposition to the established order. This may be contrasted with the more pragmatic approach of green parties in Europe, where accommodation with Social Democratic governments has moderated their ideological purity.

One of the chief goals of the Greens has been to steer Britain's energy strategy away from nuclear power and exploitation of fossil fuels. The party is left of centre in terms of social policy, but also advocates sustainable growth and demographic balance in

order to reduce resource use and maintain a more healthy balance between human society and natural ecology.

In electoral–political terms, the Greens have achieved their greatest successes competing in elections to the devolved regional parliaments in Scotland, Wales and London, as well as in the European elections. There the party has been able to take advantage of proportional representation, gaining seats from the regional vote rather than the constituencies. But the biggest success of the Greens has been to promote greater awareness of ecological issues among the main parties. Both the Conservatives and Labour have adapted to the 'greening' of politics, and both parties offer more environmentally aware policies on a range of issues, including carbon-trading, green taxes and recycling.

Note The Greens have benefited from the use of proportional representation systems in the devolved regional assemblies.

Yet there remains a *fundamental gulf* between the Green Party's support for ecology and the mainstream parties' support for environmental protection. This can be seen in Labour's decision to support the continued expansion of Heathrow Airport despite popular opposition to the project. For the Greens, who oppose growth for its own sake, the idea of expanding air travel in an age of diminishing oil reserves is nonsensical and contradictory; yet for the government — which is more responsive to the business lobby — expansion of air travel is both desirable and legitimate if it can be shown that the resulting increase in environmental pollution will remain below targets set by government scientists.

Key terms and concepts

Anthropocentrism	The belief that the world is for human use and enjoyment and has no value independent of its utility for the human race
Ecology	Science studying the relationship between living things and their environment
Ecosystem	A system of organisms occupying a habitat, incorporating those aspects of the physical environment with which they interact
Environmentalism	Form of shallow ecologism concerned solely with reforming the existing political and economic system
Industrialism	According to ecologists, a 'super-ideology' transcending traditional categories such as socialist and capitalist, where the emphasis is on 'growth without reason'
Instrumentalism	Justification for human action based exclusively on technical and pragmatic considerations
Sustainability	Principle asserting that natural resources are finite and economic growth cannot continue indefinitely

9 Multiculturalism

1 Introduction

Multiculturalism is an important theme in the Edexcel and AQA Government and Politics specifications, focusing on minority **rights**, racial equality and positive discrimination. Students must be familiar with the core ideas of multiculturalism, the contradictions between liberal universalism and liberal pluralism, the importance of identity and recognition, and the challenges to cosmopolitanism and toleration posed by communitarian and neonationalist ideologies based on cultural homogeneity and assimilation.

In the post-war era, debates on multiculturalism were stimulated by the emergence of anti-colonial movements in the developing world and the equal-rights struggles of minorities and women in the industrialised nations. This led some philosophers and sociologists to challenge the prevailing discourse of liberal equality established by thinkers such as John Rawls.

Whereas modern liberals advocate equal citizenship and universal justice, focusing on the need for consensus and equal treatment rather than diversity or specificity, multiculturalists focus on minority rights, self-determination, cultural distinctiveness and co-existence as *positive* features of democratic polities. Multiculturalists emphasise the following ideas:

- Racial and cultural identity constitute inherent and fundamental dimensions of human social life.
- Racial and cultural stratification is a persistent feature of modern societies, despite the formal equality of citizens before the law.
- Racial and cultural stratification has a major impact on the distribution of economic resources.
- The state has a duty to combat racism, support collective identities and empower traditionally disadvantaged groups.

Multiculturalists highlight the tension between liberalism and nationalism in the modern state. For this reason, it is essential for students to connect the debates on diversity and distinction in this chapter with the concepts and ideas discussed in Chapters 1, 5 and 6. The normative claims and empirical analyses of multiculturalism indicate the limits of civic nationalism as a means for reconciling formal equality and social diversity.

Key issues and debates
- **the celebration of diversity;**
- **the legitimacy of minority rights;**
- **the new identity politics;**
- **the politics of recognition;**
- **the debate between liberal rationalists and liberal multiculturalists;**
- **pluralist multiculturalism; and**
- **the debate on positive discrimination.**

2 Core ideas of multiculturalism

2.1 Diversity

Recognition of the importance of diversity lies at the heart of all multicultural theory. The traditional emphasis in liberalism on freedom of conscience and toleration allows for the peaceful co-existence of different political and religious communities within nation-states, but does little to accommodate the specific claims of minorities who possess a moral interest in preserving their linguistic heritage and/or cultural distinctiveness. Arguments in favour of diversity are based on two key claims:

- On the one hand, multiculturalists reject the liberal belief in equal treatment as politically inadequate. Cultural and religious communities have distinctive needs and preferences, which may be undermined by the strictly egalitarian demand to treat all citizens in a similar way. British Jews, for example, celebrate festivals such as Yom Kippur that are not observed by the rest of the population, but that allow Jews the right *not* to attend work. Hence the liberal insistence that religious observance is solely the private affair of individuals is unsustainable because Jewish people claim a legitimate right to be absent from work on days when non-Jews are expected to be present.

- On the other hand, diversity is celebrated because — as John Stuart Mill argued — it encourages the greatest possible flowering of human life and therefore the greatest possibility of cultural progress. Diversity is both a good in itself and a means to an end, enhancing human life by moderating the homogenising impact of modern civilisation. As a liberal rationalist, Mill believed that human communities must share basic values in the interests of political stability, but he also recognised the fundamental importance of freedom of thought and expression as defences against the 'tyranny of the majority'. Only where freedom of expression and diversity of opinion are guaranteed can democratic politics flourish.

Note For Mill, diversity was both a means to an end and a desirable end in itself.

2.2 Minority rights

Critics of liberalism suggest that while the traditional demand for equal treatment is laudable, it ignores the fundamental inequalities caused by domination. This is particularly problematic where social domination assumes a structural form, as opposed to domination in the immediate sense of one person actively oppressing another. **Structural domination** is normally concealed and can be addressed only through *differential* treatment.

A good example of structural domination is the inequality experienced by African Americans despite their formally equal political and civil rights. The category 'white' in American political culture embraces many non-European peoples, but as descendants of slaves African Americans were not included in the original definition of American political society, i.e. as equal citizens. Neither has their contribution to the economic development of the USA been fully acknowledged, which allowed white Europeans to accumulate capital while blacks remained propertyless, subordinate and dependent.

For this reason, positive discrimination has been used in the USA to address the minority rights of African Americans who, like aboriginal and **indigenous peoples** in North America, South America and Australia, have suffered systematic discrimination on the grounds of race.

Note In the USA, positive discrimination is referred to as 'affirmative action', and remains a highly controversial policy, particularly in the education system.

Minority rights are typically opposed by liberal rationalists on the assumption that they contradict the principle of state neutrality. Opponents of multiculturalism argue that it is not clear why the exercise of state power is necessary to combat **racism** and ethnocentrism. Yet these rights are defended by multiculturalists because state neutrality ignores the differential social power that either prevents individuals from disadvantaged social and ethnic minorities from participating meaningfully in society or prevents individuals from exercising legitimate forms of identification.

2.3 Identity

Identity is crucial for understanding multiculturalist ideology. Building on the achievements of liberal multiculturalists, pluralist multiculturalists insist that the assumption of state neutrality in Western political theory ignores the *actual* ways in which dominant groups in the West have used the state to promote specific cultural identities at the expense of minority groups and cultures.

The anthropologist Richard Jenkins argues that human social life is 'unimaginable without some means of knowing who others are and some sense of who we are'. The **politics of identity** have become a central problematic in Western political theory, as a multitude of new social movements — from women's liberation to the rights of indigenous peoples — challenge the traditional liberal consensus. This concern with identity is enduring, he argues, but has intensified in recent decades as a response to the uncertainty created by rapid modernisation.

Individual identity is concerned largely with problems of definition, with the *individuation* of subjects as separate and distinct beings, each defined by their own personal characteristics. Collective identity, on the other hand, is concerned with commonality, with the things communities (broadly defined) share and which differentiate them from other communities. Although distinctive, however, individual and collective identities have important features in common:

- Both are forms of labelling, which mark out boundaries of inclusion and exclusion. Assuming an identity is linked to the acquisition/rejection of given socio–cultural characteristics. Individuals acquire or emphasise characteristics that reflect their perception of status, while groups may collectively reinforce traits that support their claim to uniqueness or increase group cohesion.
- Both are socially produced, most obviously through social institutions and civic–political organisations. However, individual identities are produced through socialisation and delineate differences based on family, class, gender and community, white collective identities are acquired through a broader engagement with society, allowing individuals to identify with norms and ways of life that may be obscure or irrelevant to others.

2.4 Recognition

Following the rise of new social movements in the 1960s and 1970s, identity has become a key issue in the political struggles of women and minorities for **recognition**. The demand for recognition stems less from blatant degradation than from the vulnerability and subtle humiliation experienced by individuals who have traditionally been denied respect and self-validation. In the advanced industrial societies of the West, this has led women's groups and members of traditionally disadvantaged minorities to challenge the denial of recognition for the harm or humiliation suffered through historic injustices or structural domination.

The sociologist Axel Honneth links the problem of recognition to the achievement of moral responsibility. He argues that 'disrespect represents a historically variable quantity because the semantic content of what counts as a morally responsible agent changes with the development of legal relations'. The denial of rights to certain individuals not only undermines their self-respect, but prevents them from achieving moral **autonomy** as equal partners in social interaction and exchange.

> *Note* Absence of recognition reduces self-respect and undermines the psychological self-confidence of individuals subject to discriminatory practices.

This emphasis on recognition is exemplified by the gay-rights movement in Europe and America, which began as a protest against police harassment and legal discrimination, but grew to become a mass movement celebrating alternative sexual identities. This struggle for recognition was opposed by conservatives who feared the consequences of endorsing 'deviant' behaviour. Yet, while conservatives continue to resist calls to treat homosexual identities as equivalent to heterosexual ones, recognition of the legitimacy of alternative lifestyles has increased in mainstream society.

Liberalism and multiculturalism

To understand multiculturalism, students must consider its relationship with liberalism as the dominant ideology of the West. As we saw in Chapter 1, there is an ideological division within liberalism between those who emphasise *value-consensus* (the belief that universal agreement over liberal values constitutes the basis for rational organisation) and those who emphasise *value-pluralism* (the view that alternative social and cultural preferences can co-exist within nation-states).

The liberal reception of multicultural ideology has been mixed. Many liberal universalists reject the focus on minority rights and cultural diversity as unnecessary distractions from the more important goals of liberal equality and liberal citizenship. They suggest that multiculturalism is based on an 'essentialist' reading of culture, which overrides free association and ignores the social construction of identities.

For many liberals, culture is the private affair of individuals, and, instead of addressing minority concerns, the primary goal of politics should be to agree on principles of democracy and justice that benefit *all* citizens irrespective of ethnicity, identity or religion. This reflects the continuing appeal of liberal universalism as against *modus vivendi* approaches.

Others, such as the Canadian philosopher Will Kymlicka, adopt a more positive approach, defining minority rights in terms of individuals rather than communities. Kymlicka rejects the idea that defending minority rights is equal to embracing **communitarianism**. Some closed communities persist in industrialised nations (e.g. the Amish in America), and are usually (but not always) allowed to practise their pre-modern lifestyles unhindered. But the real issue is the extent to which public support should be offered to celebrate ethnic diversity and address minority claims.

The key question is not whether pre-modern cultures with illiberal values 'deserve' to persist within a modern, secular mass culture (they will continue to do so anyway until such time as they either decide to mix or are forced to assimilate), but whether minorities that share and benefit from liberal principles such as toleration and justice *need* minority rights over and above democratic citizenship.

3.1 Liberalism and communitarianism

Early attempts to develop a theory of multiculturalism began with debates between liberals and communitarians. All liberals believe that individuals should be free to determine their own conception of the 'good life' without interference, and support the liberation of individuals from all forms of inherited status such as religion, language or culture. In the liberal mindset, a community is simply an aggregation of individuals with different resources, each of them free to choose their alignments and loyalties in accordance with their own self-interest. Should a person no longer wish to belong to a given community, or subscribe to a particular way of life, then, as a rational being, he or she has the right to leave. Belonging is not predetermined and unconditional but *voluntary*. Communitarians, on the other hand, reject the idea of 'disembedded' individuals without

ties to particular contexts. They hold that the individual is always defined by culture and context, which cannot simply be exchanged in a free market of ideas and identities. Individuality and self-determination must be balanced against obligation and collective agency: individuals are the products of social practices as well as personal choices.

Those who associate all minority rights with a defence of communitarianism tend to ignore one of the more important aspects of modern identity politics: the majority of claims for special treatment and/or minority rights stem not from closed communities but from groups or communities that embrace secularism and modernity. For this reason, a simplistic equation of multiculturalism and communitarianism overlooks the possibility of establishing a *liberal* framework for minority and sub-state rights. This is equally applicable whether we focus on disadvantaged groups such as ethnic-minority women, or indigenous peoples who seek to establish self-determination within the territories where they constitute a majority.

3.2 Liberal multiculturalism

Professor Yael Tamir argues that the demand for self-determination stakes a cultural rather than simply a political claim, namely the right to preserve the existence of a community or national group as a *distinct* cultural entity. The task of politics is to organise a framework that facilitates recognition while defending the sovereignty and universal validity of liberal political and legal institutions.

The liberal culturalist approach of thinkers such as Kymlicka and Tamir stems from a recognition that claims based on cultural adherence or national identity can be reconciled with political liberalism *if and only if* minority rights do not contradict the principle of individual autonomy at the centre of liberal ideology. This can be explained using two examples:

- First, consider the possibility that a minority might seek to claim rights *against* its own members, e.g. to preserve control over women within closed religious communities, who have no choice but to submit to arranged marriage. In such situations, liberals could, rightly, object that minority rights conflict with the universal principles of autonomy and equality by allowing community leaders to sustain a condition of patriarchy. By preserving 'internal restrictions' over the actions of women, men within the community maintain a system of domination that is at odds with a liberal society.

Note Minority rights should not be used to restrict the rights of more vulnerable members of specific communities, who might otherwise benefit from the universal rights available to all members of society.

- Second, consider the demand for 'external protections' from a particular community, e.g. the indigenous Amerindian peoples of the Andes. Here the demand for minority rights will in all probability be legitimate because it is designed to protect the group in question from the potentially harmful actions of the majority. Not only do some national minorities and indigenous people have a moral interest in preserving their culture, they also have an existential interest in preserving their means of livelihood.

Although the claim for 'external protections' may be legitimate, many liberals still favour a centralised, neutral state, based on universal rights, to an interventionist state responsive to demands for local sovereignty and/or the reversal of historic injustices. Sceptics argue that it is up to liberal multiculturalists to prove that intervention in defence of minority rights would actually increase freedom. They seek to preserve the ideal of an impartial state, even though a completely impartial state would be possible only if no one group could exert disproportionate influence over public policy.

Liberal multiculturalists such as Kymlicka reject this assumption of cultural neutrality in Western societies because countries such as France, Britain and America all promote assimilation into a dominant 'societal culture' based on shared language, patriotism and respect for established (secular) ways of life.

'Societal cultures' may be pluralistic — encouraging rather than restricting toleration — but they are nonetheless *institutionally* reproduced and maintained through official public channels.

From this perspective, the critique of liberal multiculturalism is ideologically driven: it presents dominant identities as 'primordial' or 'essential' rather than as negotiated or socially produced. This obscures the way that dominant groups use their relative positional influence to determine norms and identities *that subsequently become binding for minorities*, and that either contradict or override legitimate identities at variance with mainstream societal culture.

An obvious example of this would be the rights of Muslims in European countries, where the societal culture is avowedly secular and intolerant of manifestations of religious identity. In France, the 'difference-blind' state ideology of the republican constitution obscures the *historically privileged* position of French culture, and creates obstacles for North Africans who wish to compete for resources and rewards, but who seek to retain their own (or their parents') native identity in a white European society.

The end-result is negative discrimination, where access to status and rewards is reduced for those who fail to embody the official societal culture. This discrimination could be reversed if the state were to balance the formal demand for equal treatment with recognition of the difficulties experienced by North Africans when competing for jobs and resources. Given their marginal socio–economic position, it is all but impossible for the children of North African immigrants to obtain the cultural capital necessary to enter the elite universities and compete for the best jobs.

Note Multiculturalists argue that assimilation in Western liberal democracies is inevitably a one-way street, rather than an open or honest form of cultural exchange.

Pluralism and multiculturalism

4.1 Value-pluralism

Critics of liberal universalism such as John Gray, author of *False Dawn: The Delusions of Global Capitalism*, believe that it is impossible for liberals to expect universal agreement on what constitutes the 'good life'. Rejecting the possibility of value-consensus in multicultural societies, Gray insists that all we can reasonably hope for is a *modus vivendi*, a way of co-existing peacefully while pursuing our own ideas of the 'good'. This applies not just to different value systems, but to different cultures and ways of living: we have to accept that ways of life that are different to the majority societal culture may seem invalid or illegitimate, but in fact deserve recognition.

To assume that liberal values are universally valid is, Gray argues, a 'relic' of Enlightenment rationalism, as absurd as the neoliberal belief that the many different types of capitalism that emerged in the twentieth century will 'inevitably' converge around the *laissez-faire* premises of the Anglo-American model:

'The belief that modern societies will everywhere converge on the same values does not result from historical inquiry. It is a confession of faith. In fact, late modern societies show little evidence of any such consensus. They differ from each other too much.'

For Gray, the concept of *modus vivendi* represents an application of value-pluralism to actual political practice. It begins with the assumption that any cultural system or ideology that claims to offer a final resolution of social and ethical conflict must be rejected in favour of 'common institutions in which the claims of rival values can be reconciled'. He thus rejects Hayek's claim that there must be a 'true' liberalism that all rational individuals would rationally accept. The assumption that the 'good life' must be equivalent for *all* individuals ignores the very real effects of cultural difference.

Recognition of the importance of ethical pluralism and cultural diversity means accepting the *incommensurability* of different values, which arises for several reasons, namely:
- the impact of conventions that govern ethical life in different cultures;
- the existence of different interpretations of the same 'good' in different cultures;
- the tendency of different cultures to honour and celebrate different virtues.

This does not mean that all incommensurable values are equally valid because direct comparison is often impossible: as Gray argues, 'affirming that some particular way of life can be compared in value with another in no way implies that all ways of life are equally valuable'. This is important, because although recognition of value-pluralism encourages relativism (the view that all belief systems are equally 'true'), it does not mean that moral reasoning is impossible.

This is so because values do not exist in impermeable compartments, closed and unintelligible to each other. On the contrary, pluralists assert that moral values that ground specific cultures are open to interpretation by outsiders who can evaluate the rationality of specific beliefs for themselves and reject *generically human evils* that would prevent any person — irrespective of cultural identity — from leading a good life. At the same time, many individuals, e.g. immigrants who retain their culture and language in their host country, are perfectly able to reason between two value systems. It may be the case that bicultural individuals will experience conflict over which values take priority, but the fact that one person is able to experience the authenticity of rival conceptions of freedom proves the inherent weakness of liberal universalism.

Note Pluralist multiculturalists deny the charge of relativism, and agree that not all incommensurable values can be equally true.

4.2 Pluralist multiculturalism and social conflict

Value-pluralists begin with the assumption that, in **cosmopolitan** and multicultural societies, the pursuit of value-consensus is not only futile but undesirable. The denial of plural identities treats difference as *deviance*, punishing those communities (or members of communities) who fail to adapt to the demand for uniformity implicit in 'societal' cultures.

In multicultural societies, the demand for uniformity leads to discrimination and exclusion. Value-pluralists argue for a 'politics of cultural difference' to take into account the differential needs and interests of communities and minority identities.

In multi-ethnic societies, the demand for uniformity can lead to intercommunal violence or civil war, where the majority group refuses to acknowledge the claims of a significant minority group for sub-state rights.

Such negative outcomes can be avoided, it is argued, where governments adopt a creative and inclusive approach to diversity by developing political institutions to accommodate demands for minority rights through 'constitutional recognition'. As James Tully, author of *Strange Multiplicity: Constitutionalism in an Age of Diversity*, argues, constitutional recognition represents 'an intercultural dialogue in which the culturally diverse sovereign citizens of contemporary societies negotiate agreements on their ways of association over time in accord with the conventions of mutual recognition, consent and continuity'.

While there are significant obstacles and dangers involved in recognising value-pluralism and cultural diversity, one of the benefits of inclusive or interventionist state projects is that they encourage members of the dominant societal culture to think critically about the validity and utility of hegemonic values and identities. Yet opponents of multiculturalism maintain that excessive demands for recognition cause instability by undermining shared societal norms and values: if too much cultural diversity and value-pluralism are allowed, then the unwritten rules and conventions that govern national life will be eroded. Citing the sociologist Emile Durkheim (1858–1917), neoconservatives stress that in the absence of value-consensus 'social solidarity' quickly disintegrates.

The retreat from multiculturalism in Britain in recent years clearly reveals the uncertainty and ambivalence felt by many native Britons towards globalisation and immigration, leading the state to respond by promoting awareness of 'Britishness' as a condition for legal citizenship. Yet this retreat into civic patriotism and the yearning for consensus fail to acknowledge the reality of life in large multicultural cities such as London, Manchester and Birmingham, where different linguistic communities co-exist in a state of mutual incomprehension: an uncoerced but imperfect *modus vivendi*.

5 Multiculturalism and politics

5.1 Challenging uniformity

Critics of imperialism argue that one of the negative consequences of the European colonial project was to reinforce Western assumptions of cultural superiority that destroyed pre-existing sovereign political customs in favour of European 'established law'. This derived in part from a failure to respect indigenous customs and traditions, but also from the immense cultural gulf separating colonisers and colonised.

This 'civilising mission' ideology clearly undermined the possibility of equal exchange between European and non-European cultures, but also encouraged a tendency towards cultural uniformity in the organisation of European constitutional states themselves, reflecting the cultural essence of the majority group. For Tully, the 'language of modern constitutionalism which has come to be authoritative was designed to exclude or assimilate cultural diversity and justify uniformity'. This can be seen most clearly in the French and American constitutions of the eighteenth century, which obliterated ancient forms of recognition based on customary law and convention. Also, although the uncodified UK constitution attaches more weight to ancient custom, despite recent concessions to regional aspirations for devolved self-government the highly centralised British unitary state is largely determined by *English* cultural norms.

> **Note** This trend towards cultural uniformity was of course emulated in many post-colonial societies, where majority groups also used control over the state to promote hegemonic identities at the expense of minority groups, with disastrous consequences.

Multiculturalists such as Tully suggest that the traditional bias towards uniformity could be challenged by allowing for a more heterogeneous form of constitutional recognition:

'Progress is not the ascent out of the ancient cultural assemblage until one reaches the imaginary uniform republic, from which one ranks and judges the less developed others on the rungs far below. Rather, it consists in learning to recognise, converse with and be mutually accommodating to the culturally diverse neighbours in the city we inhabit here and now.'

This argument takes into consideration one of the long-standing claims of value-pluralists and post-colonial theorists, namely the validity of alternative (non-European) value systems that allow for greater constitutional recognition of local and regional identities *within* the framework of the liberal nation-state, and that give minority communities a voice in national affairs or allow disadvantaged groups an opportunity to compete for status and rewards.

Multiculturalists argue that it is incumbent on states with significant national and/or religious minorities to recognise and accommodate legitimate demands for collective rights. These may include:

- *Minority-empowerment programmes* (where minority cultures are supported and promoted by using public funds, e.g. support for the Bangladeshi community by local authorities in east London).
- *Minority-language education* (where minorities can educate their children using their own language, e.g. the rights of Hungarians in the Transylvanian region of Romania).
- *Official-language status rights* (where minority languages are used in state administration and official communication, e.g. the use of French in Quebec).
- *Devolution* (where national/regional minorities acquire limited powers of self-government, e.g. the Scotland Act 1998).
- *Regional autonomy* (where power is decentralised to national/regional minorities, e.g. the Basque and Catalan regions of Spain).
- *Indigenous rights* (where historic/tribal populations acquire local sovereignty over ancient homelands against the encroaching power of the modern state, e.g. the rights of the Inuit peoples in Canada).
- *Consociationalism* (where the leaders of conflictual groups, who share a common loyalty to the state, opt for power-sharing, e.g. Northern Ireland and Lebanon).
- *Federalism* (where states pool their sovereignty by creating a higher level of government, but control their own regional affairs, e.g. Germany).
- *Confederalism* (where states share sovereignty, creating a higher level of government, but retain much greater control over their own affairs, e.g. Switzerland).
- *Secession* (where a region within a state secedes and declares independence, either through peaceful means, e.g. the break-up of Czechoslovakia, or through violence, e.g. the secession of Croatia and Bosnia from Yugoslavia).

In all of these cases, the aim of minority-rights programmes is to *manage the claims of internal minorities*, to promote empowerment and to regulate conflict — through either the introduction of sub-state rights or recognition of indigenous rights.

5.2 Sub-state rights

Note Sub-state rights are means for addressing minority claims or resolving intercommunal tensions constitutionally.

Political nationalists hold that the boundaries of the nation and state should coincide, but they rarely do so in practice. Even island nations, which have the obvious geopolitical advantage of coastal borders, contain conflictual groups, as illustrated by the long-running war between the Sinhalese and Tamils in Sri Lanka. Throughout history, diplomats have drawn lines on the map separating nations, but they have rarely solved the problem of overlapping populations and cross-border minorities. The Treaty of Versailles is perhaps the most famous example of this phenomenon, which created more problems than it solved in an attempt to deal with the complex nationality question in Eastern Europe.

Sub-state rights offer minorities the possibility of achieving national self-determination using a form of political organisation that is not a nation-state. This may involve representation rights or demands for self-government, but the logic is the same: to preserve the unity and distinctiveness of minority cultures without aspiring to full statehood. In political sociology, this type of self-determination is referred to as non-state-seeking liberal nationalism, but it can take illiberal forms, prompting critics of multiculturalism such as David Weinstock to stress the duty of states to take responsibility for those citizens whose *individual* rights may be threatened by the *collective* practices of internal minorities.

Chaim Gans, author of *The Limits of Nationalism*, argues that the majority of national self-determination movements are, or should be, non-state-seeking. National groups, he suggests, should not be encouraged to 'conceive of the states within which they enjoy self-determination as states of their own, let alone as states which they own'. Rather, the sub-state rights of national groups should be seen as a 'package of privileges to which each national group is entitled in its main geographic location'. This is distinct from the statist conception of self-determination because it confers the right to self-determination *within* a state and not as sovereign statehood and acknowledges the universal rights of homeland groups *vis-à-vis* non-homeland groups, i.e. the majority population outside a particular geographic location.

For Gans the sub-statist solution is superior to state-seeking nationalism because:
- state-seeking nationalism creates two classes of citizen within the state, namely citizens who enjoy self-determination within the state and those who do not belong to this group;
- state-seeking nationalism creates disadvantages for those members of a national group who live among the diaspora and do not benefit directly from statehood; and
- state-seeking nationalism posits the eventual emergence of a world of states in which there is absolute congruity between national groups and territorial states, which contradicts the possibility of inter-state migration and cosmopolitan citizenship.

The benefits of sub-state nationalism can be seen in the case of Spain, where the Basques enjoy a significant package of privileges designed to promote self-determination. Although this solution is rejected by separatists, whose military wing Eta uses violence in its struggle for independence from Madrid, the majority of Basque people acknowledge the benefits of sub-state rights within the sovereign state of Spain.

The same cannot be said in the case of Israel/Palestine. Here it could be argued that a dual-state solution (one that establishes Palestinian sovereignty over the pre-1967 territories formerly administered by Jordan) is preferable because Palestinians — like Arabs who live within Israel itself — cannot expect to enjoy equal political rights in the Jewish state while Israelis continue to believe that the state of Israel belongs more to *non-resident Jews* than it ever could to *resident non-Jews*.

Other positive examples of sub-state rights include the introduction of devolved authorities in Scotland and Wales, and the use of consociationalism to ensure fair representation of the Flemish-speakers of Belgium. However, political nationalists still maintain that the optimal means for defending the rights of national groups is for each group to possess its own sovereign state.

For this reason, some state-seeking nationalists demand that constitutional agreements between majority and minority groups should contain the right to secede in order to avoid the risk of war where the majority seek to harm or restrict the rights of the minority to self-determination.

5.3 Indigenous rights

The demand for indigenous homeland rights is distinct from the traditional demand for national self-determination because it employs a distinctive definition of local sovereignty divorced from the disciplinary function of the modern state. Sovereignty traditionally implies political independence, and state-centred nationalists of all colours link the development of national cultures to the effective assertion of statehood.

Note The problem of the rights of indigenous peoples raises questions about the limits of sovereignty, particularly where access to resources leads to the despoliation of historic homelands such as the Amazon.

Supporters of the rights of indigenous peoples justify their demands for self-determination on the basis of historic rights — rights that assert political autonomy while nevertheless challenging traditional concepts of sovereign power. Justifications include:

- the principle of first occupancy and symbolic importance;
- the redress of historic injustice; and
- (in some cases) the need for environmental protection.

First occupancy

The demand for indigenous rights is not designed to eliminate the rights of settlers who have colonised ancestral lands, but to assert the *original occupants'* historic right to claim. This can take one of two forms: either the claim focuses on the demographic primacy of the community within a specific homeland, e.g. the rights of expelled Palestinians who formed a majority of the population in Judaea before 1948; or it focuses on the primary importance of the territory for the history of the national group — as in the case of the Kosovan Serbs. The first justification is based on presence and entitlement. The second is based on the cultural or symbolic value of the territory for the nation in question, and is thus more difficult to assert in practice.

Historic injustice

Justifications based on redress of *historic injustice* focus on the violence inflicted by colonial powers against indigenous peoples and the need for legal restitution. The most obvious example of this is the injustice experienced by the aboriginal peoples of Australia and New Zealand: European settlers used force to take control of their ancestral lands, a practice repeated in Africa, Asia and the Americas.

Canada provides an excellent example of successful indigenous activism. There, descendants of the original Indian tribes that occupied the North American plains have organised effective strategies to establish territorial rights and achieve changes in the law. Unlike in the USA, the Canadian government has made great efforts to recognise the legitimate interests of its multiple indigenous communities while retaining its status as a sovereign nation-state (although there is some contradiction in the fact that Canadian exporters require continued access to many of the resources located in these ancestral homelands).

Environmental protection

Finally, there is the justification of *environmental protection*: defenders of indigenous rights claim that indigenous peoples may possess a better understanding of the ecological needs and complexity of ancestral lands, and that agricultural diversity should take precedence over the monolithic practices of Western agribusiness. This argument is based on the idea of appropriate husbandry. Those who are dependent on their immediate natural environment, e.g. the native tribes of the Amazon are more likely to be sensitive to the needs of the land, and therefore act more responsibly.

6 | *Can positive discrimination be justified?*

Positive discrimination is controversial strategy for addressing historic imbalances in the distribution of status positions, caused by the persistence of *negative* discrimination, bigotry and racism (factors that are perceived to have delayed racial integration and the social advancement of non-white communities in Europe and the USA because white employers routinely favour white candidates for the best jobs).

Note The debate over positive discrimination remains controversial, particularly in the USA. The success of quota-based systems of selection and recruitment is largely dependent on the willingness of majority groups to acknowledge the legitimacy of intervention in the first place.

Liberal universalist arguments in favour of **meritocracy** traditionally stress that the best-qualified candidates deserve to be given the job because they are the ones most likely to deserve the salary under conditions of resource scarcity. Meritocratic selection is also seen as the best way of demonstrating respect for the agency and autonomy of individuals. As the academic George Sher argues,

'When we hire by merit, we abstract from all facts about the applicants except their ability to perform well at the relevant tasks. By thus concentrating on their ability to perform, we treat them as agents whose purposeful acts are capable of making a difference in the world.'

According to this argument, when jobs are awarded to individuals for other reasons — whether because of racial or sexual prejudice or to satisfy ideological demands for positive discrimination — the agency of individuals is not respected, and the result is a sub-optimal allocation of resources. Clearly it is impossible to justify selection on the basis of racial or sexual prejudice, but are there grounds for *not* selecting the 'best candidate' in the interests of promoting diversity and 'levelling the playing field'?

John Edwards, author of *The Politics of Positive Discrimination*, defines positive discrimination as the 'process of discriminating by laws and policies in a society's distribution of benefits, advantages and opportunities, not by reference to individual needs, or a person's entitlement, or his deserts or merit, but by reference to irrelevant criteria, e.g. race or sex'.

Defenders of positive discrimination argue that it 'trumps' other criteria of entitlement based on formal equality or merit, but it is opposed by universalists who charge that differential treatment gives an unfair advantage to minorities that are *themselves* harmed by the knowledge that their own success might be contingent on non-meritocratic factors. As a means for promoting equality and diversity, positive discrimination is normally justified in two ways: that it compensates for historic or present injustices, and that it has beneficial consequences.

6.1 Corrective justice

The first justification is a **deontic argument** (i.e. that people should do something because they have a moral obligation to do so). To justify positive discrimination in terms of corrective justice is to argue that people should receive benefits due to special needs or some other form of special entitlement. Corrective justice has a moral basis that transcends the principle of justice as fairness, namely restitution for those (or the descendants of those) harmed by some injustice.

Critics of this argument suggest that it contradicts the principle of equality by prioritising criteria (race, class, gender) that are not functionally relevant, and thus treats people differently according to *morally irrelevant distinctions*. They also argue that collective rights to compensation for historic injustices are difficult to calculate and cause additional indirect harm to individuals who bear no personal responsibility for past wrongs: hence, individual compensation for unfair treatment is preferable.

6.2 Maximising utility

The second justification is *teleological* (i.e. that people should do something because it will maximise future utility). **Utilitarian** arguments in favour of positive discrimination assert that the 'good' to be maximised is that of the disadvantaged minority (or, in the case of women, a disadvantaged majority). There are, for example, few black or ethnic-minority judges in the UK, not because black people make poor judges, but because many black and ethnic-minority people lack the social advantages that allow white Britons to study law and rise through the judiciary. Hence, positive discrimination in favour of selecting more Afro-Caribbeans would increase the self-respect and social status of the black community, extend understanding of the law, create positive role models and contribute to the 'common good'.

Opponents of this view argue that there are (as value pluralists themselves insist) many competing ideas of the 'common good'. From this perspective, it may be rather too hopeful to expect that all sections of society would agree that the common good can be served through the special treatment of one section of the community. It is also difficult to ascertain precisely how much collective compensatory discrimination would be necessary to improve this imaginary common good.

Multiculturalists accept that the compensation-based argument contradicts widely held assumptions that corrective distribution should be awarded on an individual rather than a collective basis, and that the current generation of, say, whites in the USA cannot bear direct responsibility for the crimes of their ancestors.

However, a more powerful argument in favour of positive discrimination is that proportional quotas in the selection of candidates for jobs and educational places could be justified according to the principle of *distributive justice*. This argument can be summarised as follows:

All individuals should be awarded jobs, benefits or other specific advantages *as they would have been awarded under fair conditions*. Only racism can explain the failure of minorities to compete for and acquire a just proportion of social, economic and political goods that they would otherwise have on the basis of their actual numbers in society.

If we accept that the continued absence of proportional numbers of ethnic-minority women in the senior civil service is a function not just of lack of talent, but of *a lack of opportunity to compete effectively for such status positions due to inadequate resources*, then it follows that some form of just distribution has to be imposed at the point of selection to ensure that individuals of talent within minority communities are able to graduate from university and enter the civil service not as clerical workers but at administrative level.

For multiculturalists, the principle of fair distribution overrides the equality principle because equal outcomes are impossible in a society based on structured *inequalities* of class, race and gender. Hence, despite the resentment that may arise among the majority group, positive equality is a superior allocative principle because it takes into consideration the socio-economic (rather than purely legal) factors that allow individuals the right to compete for status and rewards.

Key terms and concepts

Autonomy	The state of being independent and responsible for one's actions
Communitarianism	Post-liberal ideology, stressing authority, common identity and cultural boundedness
Consociationalism	A political compromise based on power-sharing
Cosmopolitan	Having a sophisticated multicultural or international perspective
Deontic arguments	Philosophical arguments based on duty or obligation
Homogeneous	Composed of similar or identical parts (antonym: heterogeneous)
Identity politics	Non-class-based politics, focusing on the specific needs and interests of social groups
Indigenous peoples	Tribes or communities that claim first occupancy of a particular territory
Meritocracy	Rule by persons chosen for their superior talent or intellect
Multiculturalism	The view that racial and cultural identities constitute inherent and fundamental dimensions of human social life
Racism	Ideological view that races have distinctive cultural characteristics that are determined by hereditary factors
Recognition	Acceptance or acknowledgement of the legitimacy of a claim or right
Right	A ground for duty in others (to respect one's interests)
Secession	Unilateral or consensual withdrawal of a territory or state from membership of a larger political entity
Structural domination	Embedded asymmetries of power and social influence
Utilitarianism	Ethical theory based on the maximisation of welfare (the greatest good for the greatest number)